A SHORT HISTORY OF ENGLISH WORDS

A SHORT HISTORY OF
ENGLISH WORDS

BY

BERNARD GROOM

M.A. (Oxon. and Lond.)

FORMERLY PROFESSOR OF ENGLISH, MCMASTER UNIVERSITY

AUTHOR OF *The Diction of Poetry, from Spenser to Bridges*

LONDON

MACMILLAN & CO LTD

NEW YORK · ST MARTIN'S PRESS

1965

First Edition 1934
Reprinted 1935, 1949, 1953, 1957, 1963, 1965

PÉ
1075
.67

MACMILLAN AND COMPANY LIMITED
Little Essex Street London WC 2
also Bombay Calcutta Madras Melbourne

THE MACMILLAN COMPANY OF CANADA LIMITED
70 Bond Street Toronto 2

ST MARTIN'S PRESS INC
175 Fifth Avenue New York 10010 NY

PRINTED IN GREAT BRITAIN

PREFACE

THIS book is a historical sketch of the growth of our Vocabulary from the earliest times to the present day. By its connexions with Literature and History, the study of Vocabulary is the most humane branch of Philology; by its power to foster accuracy and taste in the choice of words, it is not the least useful. Many persons who feel an inclination to study the history of their own language are deterred by their encounter with sound-laws and the complexities of an obsolete grammar. But an interest in words as such is almost universal; our " world of words " is vast; and since the completion of the *Oxford Dictionary*, no part of knowledge is better mapped. My purpose has been to write, not an introduction to scientific Philology, but a guide to the intelligent use of the English Dictionary.

My chief authority has naturally been the *Oxford English Dictionary* itself. Of the other works which I have used, one in particular deserves mention, namely, Jespersen's *Language : Its Nature, Development, and Origin.* To this work I owe the information on the pioneers of modern Philology which will be found in my first chapter. From the same work, (p. 173) I have borrowed the convenient term " met-analysis."

I have thought it best to use throughout the term " Anglo-Saxon " rather than " Old English." I am aware of what is to be said on the other side, but it is the habit of most persons, except trained philologists, to regard " Old English " as a non-technical term applicable to any of the earlier stages of our language or civilization. This point appears to outweigh most objections to the term " Anglo-Saxon."

It is a pleasant duty to acknowledge the debt of gratitude which I owe to my former teacher, Mr. J. H. G. Grattan (now Baines Professor of the English Language in the University of Liverpool), who read the first two chapters in proof, and made several suggestions about various parts of the book, to its great advantage.

CLIFTON COLLEGE,
June, 1934.

CONTENTS

NOTE

The date in brackets after certain words indicates the earliest year in which the word is known to have existed. For nearly all such dates my authority has been the *Oxford English Dictionary*. It should be remembered that earlier records of certain words may be discovered in the future, and that therefore some of the dates may be only approximately accurate.

CHAPTER I
ANGLO-SAXON WORDS
I

LANGUAGE may be regarded from two opposite points of view. To the writer of dictionaries, words are fixed in form, meaning and function. Their connecting principle is a common derivation. All words have equal claims to respect: the common and the rare, the new and the old, the useful and the useless. The cardinal virtues of the lexicographer are thoroughness and impartiality, and we no longer expect him to exercise the personal taste and feeling in which Dr. Johnson sometimes indulged. A dictionary is a complete record of lifeless words, that is, of words in isolation.

To the imaginative writer, and especially to the poet, language is a medium for self-expression. Hard and unyielding up to a point, words can none the less be so manipulated as to bear the impress of a particular mind. To the poet, words are the work of other men's imagination, and the material for his own. "Poets," says Shelley, "are the authors of language," and his-

A

tory gives at least a partial support to this lofty claim. To the poet and his reader, words live only in a context ; in isolation their life evaporates. As for a language fixed and absolute, there is for them no such thing. The lexicographer may assume it, the mathematician may demand it, but for the poet words have neither finality nor perfection. " To seek the perfect language," says Benedetto Croce, " is to seek the immobility of motion."

But these two points of view need not, fortunately, be left in all their stark opposition. They admit of a compromise, and it is this compromise that raises the study of language from a somewhat barren science into the region of criticism and history. On the one hand, the practice of certain writers has long been recognized as a high authority for the right use of words. Johnson's *Dictionary* was founded on an extensive study of English Literature, and his method was followed, on a vastly extended basis, by the editors of the *Oxford English Dictionary*. The same view has been held for centuries by educated people : the best writers constitute in themselves an unofficial Academy. In certain regions of expression there can be no higher authority than the language of Milton, or of Dryden, or of Burke. On the other hand, our greater writers have rarely failed to learn their language in the best school, for they have studied their predecessors. The poetry of the Fifteenth Century, such as it was, was based chiefly on Chaucer; later, Spenser, Dryden and Pope served as successive models; later still, Johnson's *Dictionary*, with its definitions and its treasury of quotations, was accepted as a standard of usage; and, in more recent times, the *Oxford English Dictionary* has enjoyed some at least of the authority which it deserves. Our literary language has, in fact, long been guided and enlightened by precedent: freedom has not been lost, and licence has generally, though not always, been avoided. To divorce the study of language from the study of literature is an absurdity: each is a necessary complement of the other.

There are, however, large parts of our language which lie outside the province of literature. There is a popular English as well as a literary English. Popular words may or may not be adopted by good writers, but they are seldom made by them. Poets create many of our most beautiful words, but for much that passes our lips in the course of a day we go to other sources. The sciences, too, are responsible for many of our words; so, too, are our social habits and our political history. Again, our language has a longer continuous history than our literary tradition. In the Anglo-Saxon or Old English stage our vocabulary was, indeed, rich in poetic words, but these were the first to perish after the Norman Conquest and the ruin of Anglo-Saxon culture. In its second stage, the language acquired a literary tradition only by slow degrees : at first Middle English was mostly popular, and often tentative, in its vocabulary. The Fourteenth Century, which was the flowering time of Middle English, saw the poetry of Chaucer and Langland, the prose of Wyclif, and the emergence of one dialect to supremacy over the rest : these were great things, but the language continued to change, and in less then two centuries the works of Chaucer were barely intelligible. Only since the Sixteenth Century has there been a continuous influence of literature on language. By that time the grammar had become fixed in essentials. The unconscious or half-conscious life of the language, stretching back into remote antiquity, continues ; by its side lives the literary tradition, strengthened by criticism and scholarship.

In even a short survey of our vocabulary, then, there must be a succession of viewpoints. Anglo-Saxon must first be considered. Next comes the formation of a composite language to which Anglo-Saxon, Norse and French all contribute. This second stage is one of experiment, in which forces, conscious and unconscious, blending together, slowly produce order out of chaos. The new language begins to develop a character conformable to the genius of the race. Next comes a stage in which the national consciousness is fully awake : the vocabulary gains an ever-growing number of words expressive of the religious, political, social and intellectual life of the nation. Parallel in time to this third stage is the period of full literary influence. It is true that Chaucer and Wyclif had enriched the vocabulary with many foreign words, but such contributions are widely different from the enormous imaginative influence exerted by the Elizabethans. Since the Sixteenth Century, the vocabulary has been enlarged from all sources, literary, learned and popular, and it has borrowed from most civilized and many uncivilized languages. What of the future ? Changes are bound to come ; whether for good or ill depends largely on the number of persons who by study, reflection, and insight know the history and the true character of the " tongue that Shakespeare spake."

II

The ultimate origin of our vocabulary and its relation to other languages have been accurately known for scarcely a century. Though the Renaissance gave a great impulse to the study of words, the science of Comparative Philology is the creation of more recent times. From the beginning of the Sixteenth, until the end of the Eighteenth, Century scholars gave most of their attention to the two " classical " tongues : their superfluous time was devoted to Hebrew, which was " sacred," or to French and Italian, which were " polite." Educated Englishmen generally recognized the Teutonic origin of their language ; its older forms were sometimes studied by antiquaries ; and occasionally a Handbook on Etymology would appear, giving with tolerable accuracy the Anglo-Saxon original of many English words. But beyond this little was done, and thus, by modern standards, Philology remained unscientific. Even Dr. Johnson, with all his penetration, never knew all the truth about the relation of English to other languages ; nor indeed was the problem soluble in his time by the efforts of any one man. The beginnings of Comparative Philology were due largely to the enthusiasm for Northern or Teutonic antiquities, which was one phase of the Romantic Revival. A few students were at last prepared to leave the orthodox paths of classical study, and to devote their best energies to the early history of their own vernaculars. This enthusiasm was stronger on the continent than in England, and it was chiefly by Germans and Danes that the foundations of the new science were laid.

As far as they affect this book, the chief discoveries of Comparative Philology might be very briefly stated. A genealogical tree showing the relation of English to other members of the family of languages to which it belongs would be sufficient. But this information seldom conveys its full meaning without some statement of the evidence on which it rests. It will, therefore, be best to give a short description of the pioneer-work done by a few of the outstanding figures among early philologists. As all languages have been enriched by borrowing, it was necessary as a first step to discriminate the newer layers of a vocabulary from its original substratum. The clue to be pursued in this enquiry was suggested by a Danish philologist, Rasmus Rask (1787-1832). "However mixed a language may be," he wrote, "it belongs to the same family as another if it has the most essential, most material and indispensable words in common with it; pronouns and numerals are in this respect most decisive." This principle has, of course, many possible applications; but for the English student of Rask's time, it would yield the most interesting results by being made the basis of a comparison between English and Latin. Now some of the English pronouns and numerals, especially in their original form, evidently bear a certain resemblance to those of Latin. The Anglo-Saxon for *I* is *ic*, and for *thou* is *thu* (written *þu*). Between *ic* and the Latin *ego* there is at least a distant likeness, and between *þu* and the Latin *tu* the resemblance is undeniable. When certain Anglo-Saxon numerals are placed by the side of their Latin equivalents a similar result follows : *twa* and *duo*, *þri* and *tres*, *six* and *sex*, *tien* and *decem*. The presumption, on Rask's principle, is that English and Latin " belong to the same family," and an examination of other European languages showed that they also were members of this group. Further evidence was needed to support these conclusions, and it was found in the more or less regular correspondence of certain consonants. It was noticed, for instance, that *p* in certain common Latin words corresponded with *f* in those of the Teutonic languages : thus the Latin *pater* is the English *father* ; Latin *piscis*, English *fish* ; Latin *pes*, English *foot*. For these phenomena, which when fully enumerated make an impressive array, an explanation, or at least, a name, was provided by the German philologist, Jacob Grimm (1785-1863), who described them as a " sound-shifting." The essential points of the so-called " Grimm's Law " are that the consonants *p*, *t*, *k* (or *c*) of Greek and Latin correspond to *f*, *th*, *h* of Anglo-Saxon (as well as of other Teutonic languages in their original form), and that the consonants *b*, *d*, *g* of Greek or Latin correspond to *p*, *t*, *k* (or *c*) of the Teutonic group. The following pairs of words illustrate the "law": Latin, *p*iscis, Anglo-Saxon, *f*isc (fish); Latin, ver*t*o (I turn), Anglo-Saxon, weor*th*an (I become); Latin *c*anis, Anglo-Saxon, *h*und (dog); Latin, lu*b*ricus (older, slu*b*ricus) ("slippery"), Anglo-Saxon, slu*p*an (to slip); Latin e*d*ere, Anglo-Saxon, e*t*an (to eat); Latin a*g*er, Anglo-Saxon ae*c*er (field). Grimm's "Law" thus disclosed a half-hidden resemblance between certain key-words of the Classical and the Teutonic languages, confirming the presumption that both groups were descended from a common ancestor. It also revealed the possibility of considerable sound-changes over long periods of time. If, for instance, *pater* and *father* were originally the same word, the laws of phonetic variation might well prove surprising on further investigation.

The next step was to make out a general genealogy for the European languages; but this task could not be completed until certain Asiatic tongues were also taken into account. In 1833, appeared a book on Comparative Philology by Franz Bopp (1791-1867), whose chief study had been Sanskrit, the parent tongue of many Indian dialects. This book established the relation of the principal European languages, as well as of some spoken in Asia; in other words, it drew up the family tree of the "Indo-European" tongues. Many of Bopp's conclusions have been slightly modified, but his main views have stood the test of time. As if to prepare the world for the acceptance of new and perhaps difficult ideas, a timely pamphlet by a Dane named Bredsdorff on the causes of phonetic change had appeared in 1821. For the wide modifications in form which words may undergo in the course of ages Bredsdorff enumerates the following causes : (1) Mishearing and misunderstanding ; (2) misrecollection ; (3) imperfection of organs ; (4) indolence ; (5) tendency towards analogy ; (6) the desire to be distinct ; (7) the need of expressing new ideas. Some of these causes are still operative, even in the days of universal education. It will be readily conceived that in prehistoric times they were even more potent.

The early philologists had now proved that the origin of the Teutonic and " Classical " languages was to be found in the tongue of an ancient group of tribes living in some sort of association before their migration to distant homes in Europe and Asia. For this parent tongue three different names were suggested : Indo-European, Indo-Germanic, and Aryan. The first is certainly descriptive, and is now, perhaps, the most commonly used. The Aryans bequeathed to their descendants the vocabulary which, after innumerable modifications and additions, is still recognizable as a link between Greek and German, between Indian and Celt. Starting from the East, the principal groups of languages derived from Indo-European are (1) the Eastern group, including Sanskrit, Persian, etc.; (2) Armenian; (3) Greek; (4) Albanian; (5) Italic, of which the chief branch is Latin, from the popular form of which are descended the Romance languages : Roumanian, Italian, French, Spanish, Portuguese, etc.; (6) Balto-Slavonic, comprising among others, Lithuanian, Russian, Bulgarian, Czech and Polish; (7) Teutonic, consisting of (*a*) Gothic, the most easterly member of the group, now extinct; (*b*) Scandinavian, the parent tongue of Swedish, Norwegian, Danish and Icelandic; (*c*) West Germanic, the source of German, Dutch and Anglo-Saxon; (8) Celtic, including the tongue of ancient Gaul, Welsh, Cornish and Bas-Breton, Irish-Gaelic, Scots-Gaelic, and Manx. The languages of modern Europe outside the Indo-European family are Finnish, Hungarian, Basque and Turkish.

It is well to pause for a moment to consider the effect of these discoveries on the minds of men. First, the law of change had been exhibited as constantly at work in all languages. Doubtless, change might be for better or for worse; but henceforth it would be impossible to regard the usage of any one age or country as an example to all other times. The literary critic might still sing the praises of Ciceronian Latin, but the Latin of the Dark Ages could no longer be dismissed simply as " corrupt," seeing that it was a necessary stage in the development of new excellences by its modern descendants. Change from " classical " usage might be a sign of growth as well as of decay. Indeed the supposed fixity of the " classical " tongues was shown to be no more than a passing phase in a long evolution. Besides this, the relative importance of the Indo-European languages appeared in a new light. As members of one family they seemed more nearly equal; the proud were abased and the humble exalted. A new impulse was given to the study of the vernacular all over Europe. The comparative advantages of different grammatical systems could be judged impartially, and it was no longer to be assumed that elaborate inflexions were a mark of superiority. In a word, languages were henceforth to be judged by their intrinsic qualities, not by comparison with Greek or Latin of the classical periods.

III

Those words in Anglo-Saxon which are indubitably descended from Primitive Indo-European are of particular interest as forming the most ancient part of our language. A word which is found in most of the language-groups, eastern and western, of the Indo-European family, may be assumed to have belonged to the original vocabulary of our remote ancestors. Often enough words undergo so many transformations in the course of time that their descent from the primary root is evident only to the expert philologist. Thus, the Greek ἵππος (hippos), the Latin *equus*, and the Anglo-Saxon *eoh* (" horse ") do not, on the surface, appear to be in any way related, though they are, in fact, all descended from a primitive *ekva*. Some words, on the other hand, have changed comparatively little. The word for " mouse," for instance, has survived with surprisingly few variations. The Persian is *mush*, while Greek, Latin, Old High German, Swedish, Icelandic and Anglo-Saxon have the identical form, *mus*. Of the numerals the word for " six " has changed less than most : the Sanskrit and Persian forms are *shash*; Latin, *sex*; Gaelic and Irish, *se*; Russian, *sheste*; Danish, Swedish, and Anglo-Saxon, *sex*. Taken together, the words common to the earliest surviving Indo-European dialects form a suggestive picture of our ancestors' life at a remotely distant epoch. The Primitive Indo-Europeans seem to have been nomadic, but far from barbarous. They had, for example, names for the nearest family relationships which have descended to Anglo-Saxon as *faeder* (father), *modor* (mother), *broþor* (brother), *sweostor* (sister), *sunu* (son), and *dohtor* (daughter). They had, further, various names of animals, represented by (for example), *cu* (cow), *gos* (goose), *su* (sow), and *wulf* (wolf). Certain names denoting the necessary implements of a wandering people are of Primitive Indo-European origin, *e.g.*, *hweol* (wheel), *geoc* (yoke), *waegn* (wain). Some knowledge of carpentry among the Indo-Europeans is proved by the existence of cognates to the A.S. words *dor* and *duru* (door), *hlaeder* (ladder), and *timber* (timber), but only one tree-name can be added to the list, viz., *birce* (birch). The Primitive Indo-European vocabulary contains only one or two names of colours ; these are represented by the Anglo-Saxon *read* (red), and *geolu* (yellow). Of the original verb-system, the following A.S. equivalents are examples : *etan* (eat), *faran* (fare), *siwian* (sew), *don* (do), *wyrgan* (worry, of animals), *werian* (wear) ; of the original adjectives : *geong* (young), *ful* (foul), *freo* (free), *leof* (lief, dear), *leoht* (light), *sear* (sere).

Next in antiquity are the words which may be described generally as West Aryan. These are words widespread among the races who settled in Europe, but absent from the vocabularies of Sanskrit and Persian. The original home of the Primitive Aryans is uncertain, but the evidence of language suggests that certain tribes broke off from the parent stock and migrating westward saw for the first time the common trees and birds of the European landscape. *Bece* (beech), *elm* (elm) and *finc* (finch) are among the Anglo-Saxon words of West Aryan origin. In the new life the arts of husbandry make progress. "There is," says Schrader, "an extremely limited amount of agreement between the European and the Asiatic branches of the Indo-European family in agricultural terminology, a considerable and significant agreement of the European languages among themselves." *Mawan* (to mow) and *erian* (to plough, or "ear") are two Anglo-Saxon words which have a West Aryan source. Perhaps the most interesting words of this group are those which suggest a closer acquaintance with the sea. Whatever the cause there is no single word for "fish" common to all the Aryan peoples. A.S. *fisc* with the cognate Latin *piscis* is West Aryan; so too are A.S. *sealt* (salt) and Latin *sal*, A.S. *mere* (sea) and Latin *mare*.

Some of the West Aryan tribes turned southwards to the peninsulas of Greece and Italy. Some eventually pushed westwards to France and the British Isles, making those lands the home of the Celtic languages. Others settled in the large area between the Alps and the Baltic Sea which corresponds to the "Germania" of the Roman historian, Tacitus. The Germans are described by Tacitus as consisting of a number of tribes, great and small, differing in many details but possessing the same national character. Their language, too, had varieties of dialect, though these were evidently descended from a single parent-tongue, to which philologists have given the name of Primitive Teutonic. This language, which, like Primitive and West Aryan, is known only by hypothesis, must have possessed an active power of self-enrichment, for many words in Anglo-Saxon have equivalents in Gothic, Old Norse, Old High German and other members of the group, but not outside it. New surroundings, new implements, new feelings became part of the life of our ancestors during their settlement in Germany, and for this experience new words had to be formed, or perhaps borrowed. Some of these words give, in combination, a suggestive idea of the reaction of the Germans to their new environment, and of the progress they made in civilization. The Anglo-Saxon *storm* (storm), *scur* (shower), *norþ* (north), *suþ* (south) and perhaps *scip* (ship) belong to this period. *Cyning* (king) and *eorl* (earl) are new Teutonic words; so are *heall* (hall) and *burh* (borough, or " fortified place "). An advance in the domestic arts is suggested by words such as *hlaf* (loaf), *dah* (dough), and *gist* (yeast).

IV

In the fifth century A.D. the home of the Anglo-Saxon language was a region on the coast of North Germany. The " language " was a group of closely-related dialects rather than a single tongue, just as the Anglo-Saxons themselves were a group of kindred tribes. The break-up of the Roman Empire left the shores of Britain comparatively defenceless, and about the middle of the fifth century a westward migration of the Anglo-Saxon tribes began. Before the middle of the sixth century most of England and of the lowlands of Scotland were populated by the Anglo-Saxon invaders. Great Britain ceased to be in the main a Celtic-speaking island. In the Highlands of Scotland, in Wales, in Cornwall, and in the Isle of Man, Celtic dialects survived, but from England the language died out, except for a few words, chiefly place-names. The river-names Avon, Esk and Usk, for example, are Celtic words meaning " water." Most of Britain south of the Forth thus became an Anglo-Saxon-speaking country. The four main varieties of the new language were localised thus : between the Forth and the Humber, the dialect was " Northumbrian " ; between the Humber and the Thames, " Mercian " ; south and west of the Thames, " West Saxon " ; and in Kent and the Isle of Wight, " Kentish." The differences between these four dialects were not great, and they would certainly not prevent mutual intercourse between the various tribes. Later, the variations became much more pronounced. Traces of the original differences may be easily illustrated from

B   E.W.

place-names of the present day, as, for instance, when the northern Don*caster* is contrasted with the southern Win*chester*. "In the Ninth Century, and probably much earlier, *Englisc* was the name applied to all the Angle and Saxon dialects spoken in Britain. The name *English* for the language is thus older than the name *England* for the country." *

Anglo-Saxon was the principal language spoken in England for rather more than five hundred years. Our knowledge of its vocabulary is derived chiefly from the literature produced in Wessex during the ninth and tenth centuries, after King Alfred had given that kingdom the cultural supremacy formerly enjoyed by Northumbria. Nearly all that is best in Anglo-Saxon literature, wherever it may have been produced in the first place, has been preserved for us by Christian scribes of Wessex. The consequence is that, though the poetical and Christian portions of the Anglo-Saxon vocabulary are well preserved, many of its popular words quite possibly perished, or perhaps went underground to reappear some centuries later. The surviving literature is deeply imbued either with the spirit of the old Teutonic epic poetry or with the ideas of Anglo-Saxon Christianity, sometimes with both. Poems such as *Beowulf*, *The Battle of Maldon*, and *The Battle of Brunanburh* preserve a highly poetic

* The *Oxford English Dictionary*.

vocabulary of great antiquity ; while those on Christian subjects, *e.g.*, *Judith* and *Juliana*, as well as many prose-writings, *e.g.*, the *Lives of the Saints*, are coloured in varying degrees by religious ideas. We are largely dependent on the "scop" and the monk for our knowledge of Anglo-Saxon.

An Anglo-Saxon Dictionary is said to record about 20,000 words, and many of these have become obsolete. The *Oxford English Dictionary* records over 400,000 words. Even when every allowance is made for the increase in the number of native words by composition and other means, the Anglo-Saxon element in our full vocabulary must appear small. None the less, English is in origin and essence an Anglo-Saxon language. Many tributaries have joined the stream, but there can be no doubt where the river rises. With an effort one could still describe most of the commonest needs, acts and thoughts in words of purely Anglo-Saxon origin. For example, the sentence : " I am hungry, thirsty, weary, cold and naked : give * me food, drink, a bed, fire and clothing " is wholly native in vocabulary. Nearly all the personal pronouns, the majority of prepositions and conjunctions, many of the commonest verbs, and a large number of nouns and adjectives in everyday use are "Anglo-Saxon." In the ordinary version of

* For the form " give," however, see p. 33.

the Lord's Prayer, for instance, only six words are foreign: "trespass," "them," "temptation," "deliver," "power" and "glory." Passages of modern verse or prose, too, may easily be found in which the vocabulary contains scarcely any foreign admixture. In the following stanza from *The Lotos-Eaters*, all the words except "they," "them," "slave," "seem," "barren," "return," and "roam" are of Anglo-Saxon origin ("down" was an early adoption from the Celts):

> They sat them down upon the yellow sand,
> Between the sun and moon upon the shore;
> And sweet it was to dream of Fatherland,
> Of child, and wife, and slave; but evermore
> Most weary seem'd the sea, weary the oar,
> Weary the wandering fields of barren foam.
> Then some one said, "We will return no more";
> And all at once they sang, "Our island home
> Is far beyond the wave; we will no longer roam."

Of the family relationships, the names of all the nearest are native: *father*, *mother*, *son*, *daughter*, *brother*, *sister*. So are many of the fundamental words of thought, *e.g.*, *God*, *soul*, *life*, *death*, *body*, as well as *thought* and *word* themselves. The cardinal numerals up to a thousand are also "Anglo-Saxon." So are many parts of the body: *head*, *eye*, *ear*, *heart*, *tongue*, *neck*, *hand*, *foot*, *arm*, etc. Many objects seen on a country walk—especially those remarked by a somewhat matter-of-fact observer—have "Anglo-

Saxon " names : *house, road, ditch, barn, hedge, hill, wood, lane, stile, tree, path.* The names of most trees are native, *e.g., oak, elm, ash, beech* ; so are those of many common animals, *e.g., horse, cow, sheep, ass.* The staple foods, such as *bread, oats, barley, wheat,* often have " Anglo-Saxon " names ; so also have the better-known weapons and implements : *spear, sword, knife, spade, axe.* Many of the most familiar titles and ranks have an Anglo-Saxon source : *king, queen, earl, lord, lady, knight.* Among adjectives, those denoting the most elementary conceptions of colour and form, and those denoting the simplest moral qualities are generally native : for example, *black, white, red, blue, grey* ; *high, long, deep, great, narrow, little* ; *good, evil, kind, wise, free, merry, busy, greedy.* Of the Anglo-Saxon verbs few have disappeared, though of course there have been many foreign additions. Nearly all verbs of the strong conjugations (*e.g., sink, sank, sunk*) are native, as well as a much smaller proportion of the weak verbs (those which form the preterite by the addition of a suffix). The auxiliary verbs, *be, have, do, shall, will* are also native. It was, on the whole, the essential and fundamental words which remained. A writer of genius but without much education, such as John Bunyan, can express himself with surprisingly little help from foreign words ; and to this day the vocabulary of a young child, up to the time when he learns to read, is predominantly "Anglo-Saxon." Our Anglo-Saxon ancestors were better educated and more reflective than the words just enumerated might suggest : but their learning perished with the Conquest, and that part only of their vocabulary remained which was needed for the simpler and more elementary things of life.

V

Every language is the mirror of a nation's mind and history, and Anglo-Saxon is of much value for the light it throws on the mind and customs of our ancestors. Of the more curious Anglo-Saxon words, many have been forgotten ; others remain in Modern English, but with a meaning often disguised or weakened. Words pointing back to pagan ideas and beliefs are scattered broadcast over Anglo-Saxon literature, and some of these survive in an altered form : *e.g.*, *wyrd* (*i.e.*, " fate," modern *weird*) and *faege* (" doomed," Scotch *fey*). The name *wael* for the corpses on a battle-field has been revived in the first syllable of the Scandinavian *Valkyrie*. The rich vocabulary of mythology is well known to the student of Anglo-Saxon in such words as *nicor* (sea-monster), *haegtesse* (witch), and *eoten* (giant), but it has mostly disappeared, leaving only a relic here and there such as *elf* (Anglo-Saxon *aelf*). Certain expressions indicative of the old conviviality are familiar to readers of *Beowulf*, such as the curious *ealu-scerwen* ("panic," literally "terror as at the loss of ale"). Traces of Anglo-Saxon methods of computing time remain in *fortnight* and the obsolescent *sennight* (seven-nights).

Most of the Anglo-Saxon political institutions were swept away by the Norman Conquest, but certain technical terms have been revived for the purposes of history; *e.g.*, *ealdormann*, *thegn*, *witenagemot*, *fyrd* (the "national militia," as distinguished from *here*, "an invading army"). The legal vocabulary was largely replaced by Old-French equivalents (cf. the substitution of *arson* for the native *baernett*, "burning"), but the memory of a few ancient institutions survives in isolated words, *e.g.*, *wer-geld* (the legal money equivalent of a person's life). Probably no part of the Anglo-Saxon vocabulary has suffered more loss than those words which indicate some complexity in mental and moral judgment. The foreign equivalents are often more concise than the native compounds, but it seems nevertheless regrettable that such useful words should have been unlearnt as: *ae-mynde* (literally, "without mind") "forgetfulness"; *forseon*, "to despise"; *mod-swip*, "resolute"; *oferhygd*, "contempt"; *ofer-spraec*, "loquacity"; *onscyte*, "calumny." The substitution of words from foreign sources for such terms as these is, for good and ill, one of the chief distinguishing marks of Middle and Modern, as compared with Old, English. From the evidence of language one would infer that in the years following the Conquest, Anglo-Saxon was narrowed down in function to expressing only the simplest and rudest ideas. Government, religion and learning passed into Norman hands ; and henceforth literary English is a blend of native and foreign elements.

VI

Though the Anglo-Saxons used the resources of their native vocabulary for forming new words to express new ideas, they also borrowed the names of many foreign customs and institutions which they adopted. Contact with the civilization of Rome gave the ancient German peoples a few words which spread over the greater part of Northern Europe, but their chief period of word-borrowing began with their conversion to Christianity. Among the words adopted by the Anglo-Saxons before their migration from the Continent are *weall* (" wall " ; Latin " vallum "), *straet* (" street " ; Latin " strata via "), *mylen* (" mill " ; late Latin " mulina "), and *win* (" wine " ; Latin " vinum "). Initial *p-* in Anglo-Saxon words is generally a sign of foreign origin, and to the list of pre-migratory borrowings may be added *pund* (" pound ")

from " pondo " and *pytt* (" pit ") from " puteus." In
the same group are included a few words of a homely
character; "butter," for example, which in Anglo-
Saxon is *butere*, is derived from Latin, " butyrum,"
itself a word of Greek origin ; and " pepper " has a
similar history : Anglo-Saxon *pipor*, Latin " piper,"
Greek " peperi." The conversion of the Anglo-
Saxons to Christianity after their settlement in Britain
led necessarily to an influx of many new words, mostly
names of offices and institutions for which there were
no equivalents in the existing vocabulary. Here and
there was an Anglo-Saxon word which lent itself to a
new use ; *e.g.*, *husl*, meaning " sacrifice "—a word of
purely pagan associations—which came to mean
" eucharist," and *fullian*, " to purify," which received
the meaning " to baptize." Most striking amid this
group of words is the modern English "Easter," which
is derived from *Eostre*, the name of an ancient god-
dess whose festivities were celebrated in the spring.
For the most part, however, the Anglo-Saxons chose
to naturalize the essential words of the Church, giving
them a form under which their Græco-Roman origin
is often much disguised. *Cirice*, for example, the
ancestor of our " church," is derived from the Greek
" kuriakon " (adj. " of the Lord "); *munuc* (monk)
from the Græco-Roman " monachus " (a recluse);
biscop (bishop) from " episcopus " (an overseer) and

preost (priest) from " presbyter " (an elder). Various other Latin words were naturalized in Anglo-Saxon after the migration; examples are *profian* (" to assume to be ") from " probare," *port* (" harbour ") from " portus," and *scol* (" school "), a late borrowing of the Eleventh Century, of Græco-Roman origin. It is remarkable what a large proportion of these foreign words has survived ; indeed, no part of the Anglo-Saxon vocabulary shows more vitality than the words derived ultimately from Greece and Rome.

VII

Anglo-Saxon, as a separate language, with a soul of its own, perished chiefly from violence without, but there were also signs of weakness within. The golden age of Anglo-Saxon culture was the Tenth Century, the period of respite between two series of Norse invasions, and of a united England ruled prosperously by Edward, Athelstan, and Edgar. If this age could have been prolonged, Anglo-Saxon might conceivably have been developed into a modern language along the lines of its own idioms and grammar ; but in the following century, symptoms of approaching dissolution become strongly marked. Anglo-Saxon, in its later stages, was afflicted by what is known as " phonetic decay " : the inflexions of nouns and verbs, on which the grammar depends, became corrupted and confused. The process was partly caused, and was certainly much aggravated, by the presence in England of numerous Danes, whose language, though closely similar to Anglo-Saxon in the roots, differed considerably in its terminations. Two races, so placed, would naturally try to evolve a means of communication in which inflexions counted for as little as possible—a process which would lead to much laxity. The renewed Norse invasions, followed by the rule of a Norse king, Canute, were a further blow to the cause of pure Anglo-Saxon; nor were matters mended during the reign of Edward the Confessor, the son of a Norman mother, under whom French manners and French words began to enter the country. The words *castel* (castle) and *prut* (proud) are examples of the slight trickle from the vocabulary of France which preceded the flood. Anglo-Saxon culture was not utterly extinguished in 1066,—Alfred's great institution, the *Chronicle*, continued to be written until the reign of Stephen—but there was not a chance of its long continuance.

The building was ruined, but the bricks remained and helped to raise the new fabric. The metaphor is, on the whole, just; yet lingering here and there in modern English may be found certain idioms and types of phrase proving that the spirit of Anglo-Saxon is not wholly extinct. To our poetic style it has bequeathed the ornament of alliteration, which scarcely one of our great poets has disdained to use ; and to our common vocabulary it has bequeathed many alliterative phrases, some of which belong to the oldest strata of Anglo-Saxon. Such phrases as *friend and foe, stock and stone, might and main, kith and kin, time and tide, have and hold, fair and foul,* are of varying antiquity, but the type is Anglo-Saxon, and some of the expressions (*e.g., have and hold*) are as ancient as *Beowulf* itself. More remarkable than the survival of isolated phrases is the vindication which the nobility of the Anglo-Saxon vocabulary has received at the hands of time. From their humble and despised condition after the Norman Conquest, our native words have, many of them, risen to rank among the most poetic and the best adapted for impressive use. Thus the native *wed* has an emotional value wanting to the foreign *marry*. In producing this distinction the somewhat sentimental cult of " homely Saxon " has played only the most trivial part. A more potent cause is to be found in a deep-seated continuity of language. There is, for example, a traditional vocabulary traceable from the Anglo-Saxon versions of the Scriptures, through the Tudor translations and so to the Authorized Version. Compared with any other work of the period, the Bible of 1611 uses a pure and ancient vocabulary, and many words not of native origin though adopted very early and completely naturalized are absent from its pages. The difference in quality and association between the words which are "Anglo-Saxon" and Biblical and those which are not is felt at once by any educated person. Thus *child* is Biblical, *boy* is not; *great* is Biblical, *big* is not; *heaven* is Biblical, *sky* is not; *smite* is Biblical, *hit* is not.* The difference between a "great man" and a "large man" or a "big man" is obvious enough, and it is the Anglo-Saxon word which is kept for the higher use. Similarly, the native *heaven* has long been felt to be a more poetical word than the borrowed "sky." English writers have not often been English philologists, yet a thousand great passages of verse and prose bear witness that no words in our vocabulary are better able than those of Anglo-Saxon origin to produce the effects of simplicity, strength and beauty.

* Some of the newer words occur exceptionally in the Bible of 1611, which is slightly "modern" compared with the earlier versions.

CHAPTER II
FOREIGN WORDS IN MIDDLE ENGLISH

FOR a century and a half after the Norman Conquest the prospect for the survival of Anglo-Saxon in any form was doubtful. The integrity of the old tongue had, indeed, been lost before even the Normans arrived. The Norse invasions had brought so many foreign words into daily use, that in many parts of the island " Englisc " was already a thing of the past. There were districts where the language might well be described as Anglo-Norse. The blow which fell in the middle of the Eleventh Century was even more severe. In a short time the whole of the Government and of the Church was in the hands of the Norman hierarchy. The language of the newcomers, a variety of French, superseded Anglo-Saxon in all the higher walks of life. For several generations France continued to supply England with rulers and courtiers, with lawyers and churchmen, under whose patronage a new literature written in Anglo-Norman began to take the place of the dying literature of the Anglo-Saxons. The victory of the foreigners seemed complete. But, as often happens, the power of an alien minority in a conquered land displayed unsuspected weaknesses. The reign of Henry III witnessed a revival of English nationality, and before the end of the Thirteenth Century many men of the native race had taken their places in Parliament. English was now in the ascendant, French was declining. But the long years of repression had not passed without deeply influencing the native tongue. Foreign words had entered the language by the score, and the practice of borrowing became a settled habit. The English which emerged in the literary revival of the Thirteenth and Fourteenth Centuries was virtually a new language. It was still unsettled in its character, still susceptible to new influences, and in its whole spirit a youthful tongue. This history of Middle English extends approximately from 1150 to 1500. Out of several dialects one arose to supremacy, and became the ancestor of Standard English. To describe the new vocabulary with special reference to this dialect, that of the East Midlands, is the task of the present chapter.

I

The Norse, or Danish, invaders whose raids so often disturbed the peace of the Anglo-Saxons, were themselves of Teutonic race and spoke a Teutonic language.

The two peoples had some words in common and many which were closely similar. The defeat of the Norsemen at the hands of Alfred confined them to the eastern side of England known as the " Danelaw," but a later series of attacks ended in the subjection of the whole country to a Norse king. Canute was a statesmanlike ruler, and at his court the language of the invaders divided with Anglo-Saxon the honours of the official tongue. The influence of Norse, however, was very unevenly distributed over the country as a whole. The old language of Wessex remained almost intact; elsewhere, Norse words supplanted large parts of the native vocabulary. To this day there are local names for geographical features which bear witness to Norse predominance. The Northern *beck* (stream), *gill* (ravine), and *fell* (hill) are Norse; so are the terminations -*thwait* and -*by*, common in place-names of the North-West and North-East. The Yorkshire *Riding* is of Norse origin, and means " third." It was a fact of great future import to the language that the East Midlands were within the boundaries of the " Danelaw."

To Old Norse we owe some of the commonest words of our present language. It has even given us two of our pronouns, the words *they* and *them*, which replaced the forms descended from the Anglo-Saxon *hie* and *him*. The battle between the native and foreign words was undecided as late as the time of Chaucer, who uses the native *hem* (them); but the Norse equivalents prevailed, leaving no trace but the form *'em*, which is still not uncommon. The prepositions *till* and *fro* are Norse; so are many other parts of speech in common use: *e.g.*, *call*, *cast*, *carp*, *clip*, *fellow*, *get*, *hit*, *leg*, *low*, *root*, *same*, *scant*, *scrap*, *skin*, *thrive*, *trust*, *wand*, *want*. The rivalry between the two vocabularies is commemorated in the pair of synonyms *raise* and *rear*, the former being the Norse, the latter the English variety of the same original verb. *Give* registers a Norse victory over the native *yeve*, which disappears from use about the Sixteenth Century. Besides these common words several are worth notice as reflecting aspects of the Norse character. *Ransack* (originally meaning " to search a house for stolen goods ") is a relic of the Viking raids; *law*—which has ousted the native *doom* from ordinary use—is a memento of the Norseman's instinct for jurisprudence. *Hustings* and *wapentake* are reminiscences of Old Norse customs. In recent times, men of letters have often drawn upon the dialects for a poetic or romantic flavouring to their style. In this way various Norse words, *e.g.*, *gar* (compel), *stor* (great), *speer* (ask), *busk* (prepare), *garth* (yard, plot of land) have become more or less familiar.

II

To a stranger visiting England in the Twelfth Century, the language of the natives would have appeared a thing of very little consequence. Few continued to write it ; no one of importance understood it : it had become a peasants' dialect. The conquering race, which dominated the country from end to end in their newly-built castles, and dispensed justice in their feudal courts, possessed all the arrogance of a superior caste, and nothing more clearly marked their supremacy than their vigorous Norman language, which distinguished them from the subject-people and linked them with the proud land across the Channel, with its high crusading spirit and chivalrous manners. In all that pertained to government and jurisdiction, to war and politics, the Normans were absolute, and our language is deeply scored with the marks of their supremacy. However unwillingly, the native English were compelled to adopt many words which expressed the power and pleasure of their masters. At the opening of the Thirteenth Century, when poetry has begun to show the first signs of revival, French words are already taking their place in the new English speech, and as the century proceeds, the number grows rapidly. But circumstances were not to suffer the complete eclipse of the native tongue. In 1204 Normandy was lost to

the English crown, and those barons who chose to remain in the country of their adoption identified themselves with its interests, and as the years passed, inevitably became more English than French. In the
same century, the strong government of Edward I—
the first monarch since the Conquest to bear an English
name—began to shape the national character, and the
reign of his grandson saw the vigour of the young
nation turned against the land of its conqueror in the
Hundred Years' War. At the same time the English
language entered the fulness of a glorious youth. It is
true that French still enjoyed a great social prestige.
" Uplandishmen," wrote a chronicler of the Fourteenth
Century, " will liken themselves to gentlemen and
strive with great business for to speak French, for to be
i-told of." It is true, also, that the best writers were
introducing new French words more freely than ever.
But the language of Chaucer and Gower, of Langland
and Wyclif had nothing to fear from foreign influence or foreign rivalry. The future of the new English
tongue was assured both by its own excellences and by
the strong national spirit. In 1362 the national language received official recognition in the statute order-
ing that the use of French in the law courts should be
discontinued. " Men of lawe fro that tyme shold plede
in her moder tunge." Twenty years later the chronicler John of Trevisa records that English was ousting

French both from the grammar schools and from the homes of the gentry. " Now, the yere of oure Lord a thousand thre hundred and foure score and fyve . . . in alle the gramere scoles of Engelond, children leveth Frensche and construeth and lerneth in Englische. . . . Also gentil men haveth now moche i-left for to teche ther children Frensche." English was destined in the future to borrow as much as ever, but its borrowings were to be a sign of vitality, not of helplessness.

III

The language spoken by the Normans was a northern dialect of French, distinguishable by several features from the contemporary dialect of Paris. About a century after the Conquest, the language of the Normans began to develop features of its own, and it even adopted a few words of English origin (*e.g.*, *wodecoke*). Contact between France and England was maintained, however, and the stream of words from Northern France continued to flow. Strictly speaking, then, two dialects were in use during the Norman and Angevin supremacy, the Anglo-Norman and the Northern French. But the differences were slight, and for our present purpose they may be ignored.

Exactly how far French supplanted the native language during the Twelfth and Thirteenth Centuries is not certain, and for its use among the " villeins " the evidence is conflicting. Two things are at least clear : English stubbornly survived in the hovel, while Norman flourished in the high places. The Court consisted exclusively of French people. The judges were mostly French and the pleadings were conducted in their language. But by the second half of the Thirteenth Century, it had become the custom to draw up new laws in Anglo-Norman. Instruction in schools was given in French, and French must also have been, with Latin, the language best known to the clergy, who were bound to use these languages in conversation. Up to about 1250, Anglo-Norman was more important than English as a literary language, and more than one author of the Thirteenth Century affirms that French is intelligible to " la laie gent " (the unlearned folk). Such statements, however, must be received with caution, for another writer towards the end of the Thirteenth Century maintains that of a hundred " lewede menne " * scarcely one knows French. This contradiction perhaps marks the beginning of the struggle which ended in the victory of English, but there is little doubt that before 1250 some knowledge of Anglo-Norman had penetrated even into the lower strata of society.

*i.e. " unlearned men."

The effects of Norman rule are visible in the names of many of our institutions, but they are clearest in our legal vocabulary. Many of the old words have passed beyond the sphere of the law-courts into ordinary life. The penetration of legal terms into our vocabulary continued long after Norman times, for "Law French" was used in the Courts till the end of the Seventeenth Century. *Assize* is found in a Latin context in 1164, and among other words of approximately the same date which have passed into English from Law Latin or Law French are *arson, coroner, jury, lease* and *treason*. Among the legal words which are now used less technically are *assets, culprit, elope, embezzle, flotsam, hue-and-cry, improve, jettison, treasure-trove, rejoinder, repeal*. Several of these did not enter the ordinary language until comparatively recent times. *Elope* is not recorded until 1596 ; *culprit* made its appearance in 1678 during the trial of the Earl of Pembroke for murder.

Besides these legal terms various other Norman or Northern French words have entered into English. Some retain a mark of their ancestry in their spelling. It was, for instance, a feature of Northern French to spell with an initial *c-* certain words which in Central French begin with *ch-*. This spelling survives in the Modern English *car, caitiff, carpenter, carry, castle, catch* (cf. " char," " chétif," " charpentier," " charrier," "château," "chasser "). *War* and *wicket* have a Northern *w-* which corresponds to Central French *gu-* ("guerre," "guichet"). Memories of Norman government and institutions survive in various words, *e.g.*, *Count* (the title), *county*, *curfew*, *demesne*, *livery*, *justice*, *villein*, most of which are first recorded in Anglo-French contexts. Other words early borrowed from French have been completely absorbed into the ordinary mass of our vocabulary, *e.g.*, *corner*, *convey*, *rebuke*, *rehearse*. *Very* was originally an Anglo-French adjective ("verrai"), and the noun *duty* is of interest as having no etymological equivalent in Central French. From Norman times dates the habit of regarding French as the language of fashion. It is significant, for example, that the older trades such as " smith," " wright," and " weaver " should have native names, while *draper* and *haberdasher*, which indicate some degree of luxury, should be Norman. *Veal* and *venison* are also Norman, and in contrast to " calf " and " deer " call to mind the indignant distinction of Wamba in *Ivanhoe* between an animal when living and when dead : " he is Saxon when he requires tendance and takes a Norman name when he becomes matter of enjoyment." The Norman vocabulary had ceased to be recruited from France by the Fourteenth Century, but the influence of French was still strong, and as many new words were introduced in the reigns of the victorious Edward III and his grandson Richard II as in any other period of Middle English.

IV

Middle English was not only the passive receiver of French words, it was the voluntary and eager borrower. The Norman additions are a sign of political subjugation, those of Central or Parisian French of intellectual indebtedness. The great enrichment of our vocabulary from French life and literature lasted from the end of the Twelfth until the end of the Fifteenth Century ; then, with the Renaissance, Greece and Rome superseded France as the main reservoir for new words. French influence culminated in the Fourteenth Century ; it afterwards declined, though it revived for a short time when Caxton was writing at the close of the Middle English period.

France held the dominant position in the life of Europe during the early Middle Ages, and French was the language in which most words expressive of the new movements first appeared. In the revival of monastic life, and in the crusading zeal which brought East and West together, France took the lead. The home of mediaeval theology was the University of Paris ; and in providing the Middle Ages with its favourite reading, romances on the " three matters " (the Trojan War and the deeds of Charlemagne and Arthur), France had no equal. Many of the words which entered English during the Thirteenth and Fourteenth Centuries were of Oriental origin, but they mostly came to us through France and in a French form. The same is true of most words derived from Latin. But by the Fourteenth Century, it was becoming common among English writers to form new words direct from Latin on the analogy of words borrowed from France, a practice of great assistance to our subsequent word-makers. Thus, *concupiscence*, which is recorded in 1340, was derived direct from Latin, but had it reached us through French, its form would be precisely the same. Many of the philosophical and scientific words which became current in English in the Fourteenth Century were part of the common property of the Latin-speaking world, but they almost invariably took the form of French words.

A sprinkling of French words is already found in the rare English texts—most of them works of religious instruction—of the late Twelfth and early Thirteenth Centuries. There is often a tendency to choose a French word in preference to a native one; thus, in a text of about 1175, *serve* takes the place of Anglo-Saxon "þeowian"; *confess*, a little later, supplants "andettan." Sometimes there is hesitation; a writer of about 1210 puts *prophetes* and then adds "forcwiddares"* as a gloss. A large proportion of the new words are connected with the religious life which was now being so much developed in the monasteries. Among the early words from this source are *procession, miracle, charity, grace, passion, paradise*, which are recorded before 1200; and in the following century come *devotion, patience, comfort, conscience, salvation, sacrifice*. Various words, *e.g.*, *satisfaction* and *scandal*, which are now used in a general sense, were originally theological terms of this type: the former meant "the performance of penal acts enjoined by a confessor," the latter, "discredit to religion caused by a religious person." The practice of introducing French religious words continued well into the Fourteenth Century, and it is particularly noticeable in the work of the great Yorkshire hermit, Richard Rolle of Hampole (? 1290-1349), in whose writings is the first record of *compunction, conversion, corruptible, sanctuary*, and many more.

By the side of these austere words some of the colour and romance of the Orient were entering our language, thanks in part to the stories of the returning Crusaders. In 1237 the word *assassin* appeared in Latin, and soon penetrated into various European languages. The word is a reminiscence of the "Old Man of the Mountains" who used to intoxicate his

* Literally, "before-speakers."

followers with " hashish " before they did execution on the Christians. *Miscreant* (Old French for " misbeliever ") preserves in its strength of reprobation memories of the horror inspired by the infidel. Other Oriental words which arrive by way of France about the same time are the Arabic *azure* and *mattress*, and the Persian *scarlet*. The mediaeval passion for animal-stories, true and fabulous, gave currency to *crocodile*, *ostrich*, *panther*, *elephant*, as well as to *griffin*, *siren* (an imaginary species of serpent) and *salamander*. Our language was also enriched by many words, which, originally part of the apparatus of learned thought, have since been merged in the ordinary vocabulary. Scholastic philosophy so dominated the minds of educated men in the Thirteenth and Fourteenth Centuries that some of its terms inevitably found their way into common speech. Such words as *filosofre* (" philosopher"), *quality*, *quantity*, *sophime* (" sophism") prove that the great disputations of the age were not wholly unknown outside academic walls, and *predestination* and *necessity* entered the language as echoes from the unending debates on Free Will. There was much to fascinate the popular mind in astrology, and though many of its more crabbed terms have been forgotten, we still use the words *ascendant*, *influence*, *retrograde*, though seldom with any recollection that these terms originally referred to the movements and positions of heavenly bodies. A man was *jovial*, *mercurial* or *saturnine* through the "influence" of the planets, which at their worst could cause a *disaster*. To mediaeval medicine our vocabulary is indebted for the word *humour* (originally meaning "moisture"), and also for the names of the four "humours," on the theory of which medical science revolved, viz., *choleric*, *melancholic*, *sanguine* and *phlegmatic*. Besides these scientific words of Greek or Roman origin, the most general terms of the arts and sciences had entered our language before the close of the Middle Ages. By the Fourteenth Century the names of the seven liberal sciences were current, viz., *Grammar*, *Logic*, *Rhetoric*, *Arithmetic*, *Geometry*, *Music* and *Astronomy*. So were various terms of culture and criticism, *e.g.*, *melody*, *tragedy*, *comedy*, *history*. Whatever the ultimate source of all these words, whether Oriental, Greek or Roman, they were Old French before they were Middle English. In their totality—and they are but a small part of the complete list—they give a striking view of the intellectual enrichment of our language during the Middle Ages.

V

Besides these cultured and stately words of known pedigree, others of a far homelier kind from regions nearer at hand were entering our vocabulary. Middle English contains various words which, though not of Anglo-Saxon origin, are certainly Teutonic, and of these many are closely similar to words in use on the coast-lands nearest to our South-Eastern shores. The languages containing these words are best described in somewhat general terms as "Middle Dutch" or "Low German." As there was much intercourse in trade and at sea between the people of England and of these "Low German" lands, it was natural that certain terms should be borrowed: *mart* and *hawker* are words which may have entered English in this way. But the history of these "Low German" words is exceedingly obscure, and some may have been current in England long before their first recorded use. *Loiter, lack, marl, mud, dote, school* (*i.e.* "shoal"), *scrub, wrangle, wriggle*, are a few of the Teutonic words added to our vocabulary during the Middle English period, and in their uninteresting homeliness they are typical of their class. Somewhat later our borrowings from the Netherlands began to assume a more distinct character. In particular, we received from Holland various terms connected with navigation and painting, two activities in which the Dutch excelled. Many of these words, however, entered English in the Sixteenth and Seventeenth Centuries, so that the subject falls outside the period under survey in this chapter.

CHAPTER III
POPULAR WORD-MAKING

CHANGE and instability are not features of the modern vernaculars only; even classical Latin of the Golden Age was liable to vicissitudes, as Horace confesses in the *Ars Poetica*:

Multa renascentur quae jam cecidere, cadentque
Quae nunc sunt in honore vocabula.*

The changes to which Horace alludes evidently take place in defiance of educated opinion; for grammars, dictionaries, and the whole apparatus of learning are designed to uphold established usage. Nevertheless, the forces of conservatism are powerless to check a gradual process of renewal and decay which seems inseparable from the life of language. Apart from new words made necessary by the advance of knowledge, minute changes are constantly taking place in the language; and it would seem that no generation is willing to hand on the inherited vocabulary to its successor absolutely unchanged. A striking instance of an apparently wanton alteration is the substitution

* " Many words which have now declined will revive, and many which are now held in honour will decline."

of the noun *donkey* for the older *ass*. There is no record of *donkey* before 1785 ; yet in defiance of the most ancient usage this new and obscure word has established itself as the common name of the animal. The adoption of new words for the purposes of vigorous and lively expression is more intelligible, though to the austerely-minded such words often seem superfluous as long as they remain new. When, for instance, the word *fuss* first came into use—it is not recorded until 1701 and its pedigree is uncertain —its friends and its foes were surely divided into two well-defined camps. That this was the fate of certain similar words there is evidence to show. Thus the words *bore* and *flabbergast* do not appear until the middle of the Eighteenth Century, and that they were a joy to some and a stumbling-block to others is clear from the complaint made by a writer in 1772 : " We are *bored* and *flabbergasted* from morning to night." How and where such words originated is often a per-plexing question. *Donkey* and *flabbergast* are thought to have been adopted from dialects ; the origin of *fuss* and *bore* is more uncertain. But in one sense at least they are all new words—they are new in their rise from obscurity to popularity. Popular word-making is, in one aspect, the wider application or general adoption of words previously limited to a narrower use or a narrower area.

During the epochs of learning and culture the opportunities for word-making are naturally restricted. The golden age of the word-maker in English was the period of some three centuries immediately after the Norman Conquest. The forces of conservatism in language are education, literary tradition, and the authority of a standard dialect. Between the Conquest and the time of Chaucer these forces were inoperative. There was no education in English ; literary traditions had been violently broken ; the dialect of every district was developing more and more its own peculiarities. Never has England enjoyed such liberty of speech. Hundreds of words unknown in Anglo-Saxon appear in the sermons and romances which form the bulk of Middle English literature. Some of these, no doubt, are old native words which had escaped previous record by mere accident ; some are borrowings not yet traced to their source, from French, Low German, or Celtic ; others may, in one sense or another, be more properly regarded as " new " words. But although the Middle Ages were especially favourable to change and novelty in language, the talent for popular word-making, in various forms, is inveterate in the human race, and it is far from inactive at the present day.

I

The power of word-making in early Middle English is shown partly in the substitution of new popular words for words of older standing, partly in the creation of words to supply deficiencies in the inherited vocabulary. The displacement of a well-established noun in common use was, as we have seen, not impossible in the Eighteenth Century : it was obviously more easy to accomplish in the unsettled and unlettered years which followed the Conquest. A characteristic word first recorded in early Middle English is *cuckoo*. The name for this bird in Anglo-Saxon was *geac*, which survived as *yeke* in some parts of the country until about the Fifteenth Century. But the onomatopoeic word was evidently more popular, and in the end, it triumphed over its rival. *Spider* is a word of somewhat similar history. It is almost unknown until the Fourteenth Century, but from that time onwards it becomes more and more popular. Three alternative words for this animal were in use at approximately the same time : the obsolescent *atter-cop*, and *lop* (both from Anglo-Saxon), and a newer word of French origin, *arain*. Anything approaching a flight of fancy is dangerous in the history of language ; yet it is impossible not to feel that in the victory of *spider* (literally, " spinner ") over

D

atter-cop (literally " poison-cup "),* *lop* and *arain*, the good genius of the English language has prevailed. The victory of *dog* over *hound* is similar. Both words are recorded in Anglo-Saxon, but whereas the second is very common and has equivalents in the other Teutonic languages, the former occurs only once, in a gloss. After the Conquest the position was gradually reversed. *Dog* became more and more popular, while *hound* ultimately ceased to be a generic name and was limited in its application to a particular species of dog.

The history of these three words is typical of a gradual change in the character of the language. Its Teutonic nature was being modified into something more truly English. A change similar to that which we have noticed among certain nouns was taking place among the verbs. About the end of the Thirteenth Century, from nobody knows where, appears the verb *cut*. Anglo-Saxon had possessed two words for this action, *snipan* and *ceorfan*. The former has disappeared altogether ; the latter survives only in the restricted senses of *carve* ; *cut*, a word of very obscure pedigree, has usurped the place occupied by them as the proper word for the common action it indicates. From the Thirteenth Century onwards the short expressive words, mostly monosyllables, for which

* Or, " poison-top " ; either explanation is possible.

English is famous, begin to appear in increasing numbers. *Sob* is recorded soon after 1200, and is followed by countless other words of imitative origin, of which—to name a few—*chip, chop, clink, crash, flap, lash, lull, sniff, snore, squeal, squeak,* were current by about 1400. During the centuries when literary production had almost ceased, English seems to have undergone a change whereby its vocabulary became more homely, expressive and intimate, and the new words which begin to appear when literature revived suggest that the native speech had come into closer contact with the affections of the people during the years of adversity. One sign of the change is the increase of diminutive and frequentative verbs. These were not unknown in Anglo-Saxon—our words *flicker* and *flutter* are examples—but Middle English is extraordinarily prolific in similar verbs indicating small, rapid movements. *Babble, bubble, cackle, chatter, hobble, mumble, mutter, scatter, shudder, sparkle, totter,* is a small selection from scores of such verbs which appear between 1150 and 1400. The love of the expressive monosyllable and of the frequentative verb has remained a distinctive feature of our vocabulary, and later centuries have followed the example set by the Middle Ages. The following is a select list of words of these kinds which first appear in print during the Sixteenth Century—possibly some were current in speech much earlier : *bang, bounce, caw, champ, chink, draggle, drizzle, gurgle, quaff, sneer, sough, thump, whimper, whinny, whizz.* *Clank, coo, sizzle, slap, squabble,* appear in the Seventeenth Century ; *slobber, smash, snigger,* in the Eighteenth. The imitative words of more recent times have often a more experimental air about them, and one feels that such words as *lop,* " a state of the sea," which first appears in 1829, and even the more familiar *slosh* (1814) and *squish* (1825), have not the assured status of the earlier formations. Nearly all the words mentioned in this paragraph are native, though some, *e.g., gurgle,** are closely paralleled in other languages.

II

Middle English had the gift of improving, as well as of inventing, and a number of our words have been made more expressive by the popular love of vivid language. Change is not necessarily for the better, and the transformation of the Anglo-Saxon *sprecan* into the Middle English *speken* may be due equally well to a sense of euphony or to laziness in pronouncing the letter *r*. But many changes were certainly made in accordance with a sense of onomatopoeic or symbolic appropriateness. One example is the word

* Cf. Italian *gorgogliare.*

sneeze, of which the initial letter has been altered from *f*. The change, it is true, may have been due in the first place to a scribal error, but the mistake having been once made there was small chance for the survival of a word legitimately descended from the A.S. *fneosan*. Another example is *simmer*, of which the original form was the less appropriate *simper*; and of other changes equally happy there are scores of examples. The evolution of *chirp* (1440) from the earlier *chirk* and *chirt* is typical : no one can doubt that this third attempt at word-making is the best. Towards the end of the Middle Ages various words first appear in the form we now use, perfected from the furnace of experiment. The following note in the *Oxford English Dictionary* on the word *clash*, first found about 1500, is significant of a very general process : " The initial element is that of *clap*, *clack*, etc., the final that of *dash*, *splash*, *smash*, etc. *Clash* thus suggests an action produced in the same way as a *clap* or *clack*, which, instead of ending abruptly like these, is broken down as it were into a mingled mass of smashing or rustling sounds." The experience of generations acting together with a sense of symbolic sound has enriched our vocabulary with many expressive words. Simple onomatopoeia, as illustrated in such words as *quack*, *caw*, and *coo*, seems to be often attainable at the first attempt; but symbolism, which is suggestive rather than imitative, subjective rather than objective, is often of slower growth. *See-saw*, " a reduplicating formation symbolic of alternating movement," seems, however, to be a ready-made instance of this kind of word ; so, also, does *zigzag*. Certain symbolic words only reveal their full character when they are grouped together ; and to form such a group one may have to collect examples from many different sources. For instance, the words beginning with *gr-* expressive of anger, disapprobation, contempt, or some such emotion form a considerable list, but they are of origins so different (Anglo-Saxon, Low German, French) that one can only assume the symbolism to be based on a very general sense. *Grim, groan, growl, grumble, grudge, gruff, gruesome, grumpy*—all seem members of the same family; and we might add to the list the more recent *grouse*, a piece of military slang. On the other hand, so many words beginning with *sl-* indicating some form of disparagement are of doubtful origin, that we may perhaps assume them to be the product of symbolic word-making in comparatively recent times. *Slag, slam* (" an ill-shaped person "), *slang, slattern, sleazy* (" flimsy "), *slouch, sloven, slum, slur, slut*, appear within the dates 1402 to 1812, and are of popular or doubtful origin. Some symbolism seems to have been produced by the modification of words already existing. A good example is *scrag*, an altered form of " crag," the change being due, according to the conjecture of the *Oxford Dictionary*, " to some feeling of ' phonetic expressiveness.' " Similarly, *scrawl* is an altered form of " crawl." Phonetic symbolism is also seen in such modifications as *chip* from *chop*, to indicate a smaller, sharper movement; *screech* from *scritch*, to suggest a more drawn-out cry; *flop* from *flap*, to indicate a duller and heavier sound. Symbolic words are sometimes invented before they are needed for any definite purpose, their appropriate use being left for time to reveal. Thus *slouch*, which is first recorded in 1515, was frequently used for about two centuries after its invention " as a term of disparagement without precise significance." *Swagger* has a similar history : it was noted, by Chapman in 1598, as a highly popular word, but it was used somewhat vaguely before its present significance was settled. When *humbug* first appeared a writer remarked in 1751 : " Some men deceive themselves so egregiously as to think they mean something by it." Symbolism seems also to have played a part in the creation of various composite words, such as *scratch*, a mixture of the obsolete " scrat " and " cratch "; *flurry*, a mixture of " flaw " and " hurry "; and *snarl*, a mixture of " snar " and " gnarl." *Flounder* is thought to be a " blending of the sound and sense of various earlier words : cf. ' founder,' ' blunder,' and the many words with initial *fl-* expressing impetus and clumsy movements." The years between the latter part of the Middle English period and the Elizabethan age seem to have been the time most favourable to symbolic word-making, but the process has never wholly ceased. In recent years, for instance, " Lewis Carroll " has provided us with several symbolic words, such as *galumph*, a mixture of " gallop " and " triumph."

III

The shortening of words by the omission of sounds from the beginning, middle or end, is one of the most general forms of change in language. The reduction of the six syllables of the Greek *eleemosune* to three in the Anglo-Saxon *aelmesse*, and to one in the Modern English *alms* is merely a striking example of a general process. Periods of barbarism and civil disturbance hasten the tendency to shorten words, just as periods of culture and education resist it. But the impulse to abbreviate is all but universal, especially in rapid and colloquial speech, and there are few persons who scruple to say *don't*, *won't*, etc., on ordinary occasions, even though greater formality is sometimes requisite.

English contains various words surviving from the different periods which have been particularly given to shortening. In the period of Middle English there was a common habit of the shortening-process which is called " aphesis," *i.e.*, the gradual and unintentional loss of a short unaccented vowel or syllable at the beginning of a word. An early example of aphesis is Modern English *spice*—a shortening of Old French " espice "—first found about 1225. *Sample* from " ensample " is recorded in 1300, and to the same date belongs *size*, from " assize," used first in the sense of " ordinance," later of " fixed standard." A little later come *fence* from " defence " and *splay* from " display " (both about 1330). From Middle English, also, come *spite* from " despite " and *sport* from " disport," and from the Sixteenth Century, *ticket* from "etiket." Other aphetic words are *cheat* from " escheat "; *chord* (with intrusive *h*) from " accord "; *spend* from " dispend "; *tire* from " attire "; *venture* from " adventure "; *vie* from " envie." The number of aphetic words produced in later times is much smaller : two examples from the Eighteenth Century are *cute* from " acute," and *lunge* from " allonge."

The practice of shortening words by " apocope," *i.e.*, the omission of final syllables, belongs to a different phase of linguistic history. It is true that apocope was in progress through the whole period of transition from Anglo-Saxon to Modern English, but it was not until later that particular words in our vocabulary began to appear as a result of the process. Shortening becomes common in the Seventeenth Century, apparently as an affectation of smartness. One of the earliest examples is *cit*, an abbreviation for " citizen " (first recorded in 1644), a much-favoured word in Court circles during the Restoration. *Miss* from " mistress," *mob* from " mobile vulgus," and *hack* from " hackney " appear between 1660 and 1700, and shortly after come *confab* from " confabulation," *chap* from " chapman," *hipps* from " hypochondria," *phiz* from " physiognomy." The rage for abbreviation was at its height in the reign of Queen Anne, and it provoked an essay from Swift who attacked the practice as a dangerous corruption of the language. Of the words mentioned by Swift, some have been retained, some lost: for instance, we no longer say *plenipo* for " plenipotentiary " ; but shortening has continued to add various words to the vocabulary. Two examples which established themselves during the Nineteenth Century are *cab* from " cabriolet," and *navvy*, a name given to the workmen employed on Internal Navigation. Some recent shortenings have remained colloquial, *e.g.*, *bike* and *photo*.

The process sometimes called " metanalysis " is responsible for adding several words to our language which are etymologically incorrect in form. We are all familiar with the habit of running two words together, as in the pronunciation of " At home " as *atome*. This habit is an old one : indeed, the very phrase " at home " is found in Middle English, spelt " atom." Metanalysis is the name given to the incorrect division of two words pronounced as one : thus *an ewt* wrongly divided gave *a newt* ; *a nadder* and *a napron* became *an adder* and *an apron* ; *an eke-name* (*i.e.*, extra name) gave *a neke-* (later *nick-*) *name* ; *a noumpere* (*i.e.*, an arbitrator) gave *an oumpere* or *umpire*. *Orange* has lost the initial *n-*, which it possesses in Spanish though not in French. *Whitsun* is due to the erroneous division of *Whit-Sunday* into *Whitsun-day*. The initial letter of *tawdry* is really the final letter of *Saint*; Saint Audrey being associated with lace and finery : once a well-known figure in England, she is now scarcely remembered save by the disparaging adjective in which her name is concealed.

A curious and not unfruitful source of additions to the vocabulary is the popular process of word-creation known as " back-formation." The term is used of the evolution of a new word from an erroneous notion as to some part of speech. There is no better instance of the process than the verb *sidle*, which is due to the supposition that " sideling "—the older word of the two—is a present participle, though it is in fact

an adverb, meaning " with a sideward movement."
The development of the verb *grovel* from the adverb
" grovelling " is precisely similar. *Grovel* appears towards the end of the Sixteenth, *sidle* towards the end
of the Seventeenth, Century ; but scattered instances
of back-formation occur earlier in the history of the
language. Thus *cherry* is a noun dating from the
Fourteenth Century, and is really a quasi-singular
form of " cherise," mistaken for a plural noun. *Pea*,
which appears in the Seventeenth Century, is a similar
formation from " pease," and *marquee* (1690) is an
assumed singular of " marquise." Other examples of
back-formation appear at various dates, and some are
quite recent. The termination *-er* or *-or* in a noun has
sometimes been wrongly apprehended as a sign of the
agent, and through this mistake several new words
have been added to the language. For example, *waft*
(1513) of which the earlier meaning was " convoy " is
a back-formation from the obsolete " wafter," *i.e.*, " an
armed vessel employed as a convoy." *Scavenge* (1644)
is a back-formation from " scavenger "; *swindle*
(1782) from " swindler "; *edit* (1792) from " editor."
These words have been fully adopted into the language,
and few persons who use them are aware of their
origin. Some back-formations, however, seem due to
a deliberate playfulness in word-making. *Resurrect*,
for instance, is sometimes used as a mild joke ; and

the American *enthuse* had a colloquial or humorous origin. It is possible that the process of back-formation provides the clue to the puzzling word *fog*, which may have developed from an adjective " foggy," meaning " murky."

IV

A part of our vocabulary about which etymology is largely in ignorance is its slang. Yet slang has added so many words to our language that the subject cannot be wholly omitted. *Slang* (which is itself a slang word) is not recorded until 1756, but the thing itself was a good deal older and was generally known as thieves' or rogues' cant. Many slang words are quite probably of arbitrary formation, being designed to form a secret language for use by persons engaged in unlawful pursuits. Many cant words in English can be traced back to Tudor times, when the underworld of rogues was beginning to be explored as a fruitful subject by literary men. *Cheat*, originally used as a synonym for " a stolen thing," and *filch* are both words from the vocabulary of thieves ; they are first recorded in the Sixteenth Century. Canting terms excited a good deal of interest in the Seventeenth Century, and it was naturally to the advantage of law-abiding persons that the language of thieves should not be wholly unknown. Several vocabularies of cant terms were published, such as the anonymous *Dictionary of the Canting Crew* which appeared about 1700. Grose's *Dictionary of the Vulgar Tongue* (1785) was the most famous collection of the Eighteenth Century. From the Restoration onwards, slang and cant words have gradually filtered into the ordinary English vocabulary, and while some have kept the flavour of their disreputable origin, others have become respectable and, in some instances, indispensable members of our vocabulary. *Quod*, for instance, as a synonym for prison, is very commonly known, though it is seldom used except in jest ; but *flog, sham* and *fun*, though originally cant terms, have been admitted into the ordinary vocabulary.

The following selection of words from *A New Canting Dictionary* is a good illustration of the fluctuations of language. The work was published in 1725 and was intended to aid " an honest man " in discovering the " profession and intentions " of suspicious persons. Among its definitions are : *bet*, " a wager " ; *bilk*, " to cheat or deceive " ; *cove*, " man, fellow, also rogue " ; *fun*, " a cheat, or slippery trick " ; *jilt*, " a tricking woman " ; *kid*, " a child " ; *nabb'd*, " taken or arrested " ; *pinch*, " to steal " ; *prig*, " a thief, a cheat " ; *scum*, " the riff-raff " ; *shabby*, " in poor, sorry rigging " ; *spark*, " a spruce, trim, gay fellow " ; *swop*, " to barter " ; *trip*, " a short voyage." These expressions are still known to-day, though some have altered their meaning, while others have lost all trace of their cant origin. The word *donkey*, already mentioned as a remarkable instance of the power of colloquial language to force its way into general use, is first recorded in Grose's *Dictionary of the Vulgar Tongue* (1785).

Some slang words, *e.g.*, *cheat*, which is a shortening of " escheat," are the degenerate offspring of well-born parents ; but it is possible that a few are original root-creations. The faculty of forming new roots has, indeed, never been lost ; though there is always something mysterious in the general adoption of words which are utterly without connections in the existing vocabulary. The American *stunt* is a recent example : there are various other words, now merged in the common mass, which are also of unknown origin, and may be described as the " foundlings of language." *Beach*, *blight*, *pet*, and *dudgeon* (in the sense of " resentment ") are among the words of which philology can render no account. Other words which may be grouped with these as equally unconnected though less mysterious are those which have been arbitrarily formed from time to time to designate some entirely new object. *Gas* was formed by the Dutch chemist Van Helmont as a kind of variant or reminiscence of " chaos," or perhaps of " Geest "

(Dutch for " spirit ") ; in more recent times *kodak* has been arbitrarily formed by Mr. George Eastman. Utterly arbitrary " trade-names " are of course being created every day, but, as Johnson remarks, " Of the laborious and mercantile part of the people the diction is in a great measure casual and mutable ; many of their terms are formed for some temporary or local convenience, and though current at certain times and places are in others utterly unknown." Most of such " words " have obviously no real status in the language.

V

As language is the creation of erring mortals, it is natural that many words should betray the results of carelessness or ignorance. It is, however, a law of language that when all men err they cease to err : a general change is a legitimate one. Words which can be labelled as out-and-out mistakes are uncommon, and occur only in somewhat peculiar circumstances. One of the few examples of a sheer blunder is the word " helpmeet," which arose out of a popular misapprehension. The sentence from Genesis ii. 18, " I will make him an help meet for him," gave rise to the notion that the two words " help meet " were a synonym for " wife," and in this way a new word—usually employed in perfect good faith—was added to the language. *Scapegoat* is another Biblical word formed in error ; the immediate source is the translation of Tindale, who misunderstood the Hebrew word Azazel (Leviticus xvi, 8) : the Revised Version has restored Azazel to the text, explaining it in the margin as " dismissal." Imperfect knowledge is responsible for most of the words which may be fairly described as erroneous or corrupt in form. False etymology is a cause of various mistakes. One of the most amusing instances is the spelling of *posthumous*, in which the *-h-* is due to the faulty derivation of *postumus* (Latin for " last ") from *post* and *humus*. The spelling *shamefaced* is due to a similar error, the correct form being " shamefast," *i.e.*, " modest," " rooted in shame." The spelling of *admiral* is another instance, this word being really derived from the Arabic " amir al," *i.e.*, " the commander," not from Latin " admirari." Misapprehension also accounts for the word *salt-cellar*, of which the second element was originally " saler," *i.e.*, a " vessel for salt," so that the addition of " salt " is superfluous. The spelling of *hiccup* as *hiccough* is due to the supposed connection of this imitative word with " cough." Analogy is another cause of erroneous spelling. The *-l-* in *could*, for instance, is etymologically incorrect : it has been added to the older *coud* by analogy with the form of "should" and " would." Beside these intelligible mistakes may

E

be placed certain words which popular misapprehension has transformed more grossly. The form of *pediment* is a flagrant example. It is derived from an older *peremint*, which is itself apparently a corruption of *pyramid*. So striking a change is, presumably, due to the mispronunciation of the word by working-men. The Elizabethan *kickshaws* is a popular distortion of the French " quelque-chose," and a possible explanation of the expression *so-long* is that it is a sailors' corruption of " salaam."

VI

Popular word-formation has played a large part in the growth of our vocabulary, and it is natural to ask whether the process survives in any form and is likely to operate in the future. Education has, of course, put an end to the more ignorant forms of word-making, but the practice itself is by no means dead : it may indeed be argued that it is dangerously active. Many writers of prose and verse, especially of the more advanced kind, feel themselves free to add to our vocabulary any " word " that they may create on the spur of the moment, with the result that novelty is beginning to lose its effect through excessive use. A certain writer may wish to convey the effect of a particular falling sound for which " splash " is the accepted word. But " splash " may appear too unlike the

sound to be suggested; and remembering that
" splosh " came into use not long ago to indicate a
heavier, clumsier fall, our author boldly writes
" splish " or " splush " according to the sound he de-
sires to echo. In theory the practice is justified, for our
language has been much enriched by this very process.
But, carried to excess, word-making of this kind would
lead first to confusion, then to anarchy. The medium
of expression is language, and language consists not of
sounds but of words, *i.e.*, of sounds assigned to certain functions by general consent. It is better to use
words as sounds than to use sounds as words. An
illustration of the difference may be provided by a
comparison of a pair of passages from two strongly-
contrasted poets. Tennyson, a great artist in words,
elicits the full sound-value from the word " pattering "
in the following lines :

> Calm is the morn without a sound,
>   Calm as to suit a calmer grief,
>   And only thro' the faded leaf
> The chestnut pattering to the ground.

Browning, a more dramatic writer, but an inferior
artist, wishing to express an intensity of rage and dis-
gust, breaks through the bounds of language and
writes down an inarticulate cry which is no word at all :

> Gr-r-r—there go, my heart's abhorrence !

For once, an eccentricity like this provokes a smile
and may pass. But one cannot help regretting at the
same time that so great a poet should have taken even
this small step towards degrading a language amply
supplied with words expressive of almost every feeling
and sensation.

CHAPTER IV

STANDARD ENGLISH AND THE DIALECTS

I

THE most important event in the history of Middle English is the emergence of one dialect to a position of supremacy over the rest. During the Thirteenth and Fourteenth Centuries, the confusion of dialects was extreme, while at the same time the growing sense of nationality, fostered by such kings as Edward I and Edward III, pointed to the need of a standard literary language. This result took a long time to achieve, but by about 1500 the process was complete. The end was attained largely by impersonal forces, but in so far as it was due to men, the greatest credit must be given to Chaucer and to Caxton. Chaucer gave East Midland its literary prestige ; * and in that dialect the first English books were printed at Caxton's press. It is significant that Caxton lived in the reign of Henry VII, for the work of the two men was analogous. Henry put an end to feudalism in government, Caxton helped

* Chaucer's dialect, though predominantly "East Midland," contained some elements from other districts.

to put an end to localism in language. Of course, the dialects outside the East Midland long survived the Fifteenth Century, nor have they wholly disappeared even yet. But after 1500 there was no longer any doubt which of the many forms of English would survive as the literary language. Standard English had come into being, and henceforth " dialect " was a word denoting something inferior, or at least provincial.

The dialects of Middle English sprang from the dialects of Anglo-Saxon. Just as in Alfred's time there were divisions of language corresponding to Northumbria, Mercia, Wessex and Kent, so in Chaucer's time there were the Northern, Midland, Southern and Kentish dialects. During the intervening years the gulf between the dialects had widened ; a Yorkshireman's speech would sound more foreign in Sussex three centuries after the Conquest than it had done two centuries before. Moreover, the number of dialects had apparently increased. * The language of the Midlands differed so much at its extremities as to form two distinct varieties of English, the East Midland and the West Midland. There was a local grammar, a local spelling, and a local vocabulary. In Newcastle, for instance, a contemporary of Chaucer would say *we singes* ; in Oxford, *we singen* ; in Southampton, *we singeth*.

* It is possible that there were more Anglo-Saxon dialects than are preserved in the records.

Every region had its own system of vowels : the North would say *mare*, and the South *more*. In vocabulary the divergences were infinite. Whereas, in the counties of the Danelaw, Norse words abounded, the language of the South-West was in origin, principally, Anglo-Saxon. French words were scattered over the kingdom in differing proportions owing to all sorts of local causes. Words peculiar to the region, whether formed locally or borrowed from abroad, swarmed in all dialects. Uneducated persons from different parts must often have found it impossible to communicate. Chaucer seems to have understood the Northern dialect, but to have found it outlandish.

This chaos could not continue indefinitely. By the end of the Fourteenth Century, East Midland had attained the literary excellence which helped to assure its final supremacy ; but localism died hard during the Fifteenth Century, and it was not until the Battle of Bosworth that the victory of the monarchy over the barons made the disorders of dialect seem an impossible anachronism. Political considerations would probably have been enough by themselves to give the dialect of London some of the status of " Standard English "; but fortunately the dialect of London was, with a few differences, the dialect of Chaucer ; it was also the dialect of the two Universities. The forces of

Court and capital, of literature and of learning, were thus united in favour of East Midland—a combination against which no rival dialect had any chance. An author of the Fourteenth Century would use the grammar and vocabulary of the English spoken in his own locality : the author of *The Pearl*, for example, writes in the rich but difficult dialect of the West Midlands. An author of the Sixteenth Century would normally take pains to acquire the pure English of the Court and capital. Of course, the change took long to effect, but for centuries the tide flowed uninterruptedly in favour of " Standard English." All over the country, the speech of educated men approximated more and more. After the accession of James I, the English of the Court began to find favour even in the more polite circles of Scotland.

It is sometimes asked, rather foolishly, whether there is, after all, such a thing as " Standard English," and much is made of slight divergences in the pronunciation of certain words in different parts of the country. It is true that we have not in Britain a completely standardized pronunciation, or even a completely standardized vocabulary. But not to know that the correct English which educated people endeavour to write and speak to-day is in all essentials descended from the English of the East Midland Counties, and not from that originally spoken in Devonshire or Shropshire, in Yorkshire or Midlothian, is to be ignorant of one of the plainest facts in history. The "broad Scots" of Burns's poems is a genuine variety of Northern English ; the Dorset dialect used by William Barnes is a true descendant of Southern. But what educated person to-day speaks as either of these poets wrote ? That the dialects were not extinguished after 1500 is, however, a fact hardly less important. They became more provincial, more rustic ; many lost their purity and developed unhistorical features. But many parts of the country have kept good dialect words of ancient descent ; and of these some have found their way into "Standard English," especially through the works of such men as Burns, Wordsworth and Scott. The enrichment of "East Midland" from the resources of its sister dialects is a matter of no small importance to the history of the English vocabulary.

II

The importance of Chaucer in the history of our language has always been recognized. To the men of the Sixteenth Century he was the "well of English undefiled." The vitality of his works caused them to be read even in parts of the country where the dialect was least familiar. Fifteenth Century Scotland was rich in poets of merit, but most of them were the disciples of

Chaucer, and are often known as " the Scottish Chaucerians." In England there was a dearth of poetic talent between the death of Chaucer in 1400 and the rise of Spenser about 1579. Through the whole of the Fifteenth Century and after, therefore, Chaucer's dialect enjoyed a literary prestige which no other dialect could rival.

But Chaucer also conferred benefits on East Midland in a more direct manner. He enriched its vocabulary with many terms of philosophy and science, and with many new abstract words which have since become indispensable. That he actually introduced all the words which are first recorded in his works is of course improbable, but he certainly did much to make East Midland the fittest instrument among the English dialects for the expression of ideas and the diffusion of thought and culture. The following is a select list of the words not yet found in any text earlier than the writings of Chaucer ; the majority are derived from French or Latin, a few are from Greek and Arabic :

administer, admonition, adorn, adulation, adverse, agree, alembic, almanac, alter, ambassador, apoplexy, arrogant, aspect, attention, cadence, captive, casual, centre, celestial, coagulate, commit, composition, complain, conjunction, conserve, contumely, consolation, corollary, corrosive, create, credible, delicacy, deluge, duration, edifice, elevate, elixir, erect, funeral, habitation, lethargy, persevere, perturb, position, remorse, reply, report, re-

press, resist, resolve, retain, return, rigour, sensible, transitory, tragedy, vacation, vital, vulgar, voluptuous. The list, which might easily be doubled, at least suggests the character of Chaucer's additions to the vocabulary. No other writer did so much to enrich the East Midland dialect; but the work of Chaucer's contemporary Wyclif is too important to be overlooked. Wyclif's contributions, as one would expect, mostly relate to religion and theology. The following examples are typical : *allegory, apostasy, ceremony, communion, concession, concourse, represent, retribution, transmigration, ʒeal.* Wyclif died in 1385, Chaucer in 1400. The victory of East Midland was assured, but it was not yet complete. Many details remained to be settled, and ninety years later Caxton was still hesitating between two rival words with the same meaning. His story of the merchant becalmed off the Foreland is one of the few passages which give a vivid glimpse into the early history of our language. " A mercer cam in to an hows and axed for mete, and specyally he axyd after eggys. And the goode wyf answerde that she coude speke no Frenshe. And the marchaunt was angry, for he also coude speke no Frenshe, but wolde have hadde egges, and she vnderstode hym not. And thenne at laste a nother sayd that he wolde have eyren. Then the good wyf sayd that she vnderstod hym wel. Loo ! what sholde a man in thyse dayes now wryte, egges or eyren?"* This incident, which is recorded in 1490, is a good illustration of the difficulties to be overcome before even the foundations of standard literary usage could be laid. The word which has survived (eggs) is in fact of Norse origin; the native word (eyren) seems to disappear from the written language soon after Caxton's time.

III

From the position of East Midland, fringed as it was with an inner border of English, and an outer border of Celtic dialects, it is natural that words from these sources should from time to time have penetrated into its vocabulary. The small number of Celtic words which found their way into the English language in earlier times has always been a cause of surprise to philologists. A few names of geographical features, e.g., *coomb* (a small valley), *crag*, and perhaps *down* (a hill) and *tor*, together with about half-a-dozen other words, e.g., *bin* and *dun*, make up the total known contribution of Celtic to English until about 1300. In more recent times various causes, literary, political and social, have somewhat increased the number of imported words : Irish and Scotch Gaelic in particular have been contributors, Welsh to a much smaller

* The varieties of spelling in this passage illustrate the uncertainty of usage in Caxton's time.

extent. " Standard English " has also been enriched from the other English dialects, sometimes through the medium of books, sometimes through the more obscure processes of " popular " influence.

The historic dialects of Anglo-Saxon and Middle English differed from each other in certain well-defined features of spelling and pronunciation. Relics of these ancient distinctions are preserved in the form of a few words which have entered " Standard English," displacing the normal East Midland spelling. Our adjective " left," for example, preserves in its spelling and pronunciation the characteristic of the Kentish dialect, in which the vowel *e* commonly stood for the normal *y*. The letter *y*, which in Anglo-Saxon was pronounced like the French *u* or German *ü*, was gradually " unrounded " to an *i*; but in place of *lift*, the normal development in East Midland from the older *lyft*, we have, by one of these anomalies common in the history of language, adopted the Kentish form of the word. Many of the apparent irregularities in our spelling are due to ancient distinctions of dialect. The word *build*, for example, is a composite of the Southern and the East Midland derivatives from the Anglo-Saxon *byldan*. In Southern England, where French influence was particularly strong, it was natural to spell the word *buldan*, as the French *u* corresponded in sound to the Anglo-Saxon *y*.

But in the East Midland area, as we have seen, *y* developed into *i* : and the curious spelling *build* is thus a combination of the Southern *buld* and the East Midland *bild*. Still more curious are the form and pronunciation of *-bury*, the termination of certain place-names ; for *-bury*, which is derived from Anglo-Saxon *byrig*,* has the Kentish pronunciation (*y* producing *e*), combined with the Southern form (*y* spelt as *u*). There are also a few traces of the old Northern forms. One of the most striking features of the Northern dialect is the retention in spelling of the Anglo-Saxon *ā*, which in Midland and Southern developed into *ō* (cf. Scottish and North-English *bane*, *stane*, etc., with Midland and South *bone*, *stone*). This dialectal peculiarity is found in the adjective *hale*, the northern equivalent of *whole* (the initial *w-* is unetymological), both words being derived from Anglo-Saxon *hāl*. *Raid* and *road* are another pair similarly contrasted, the former being the Northern, the latter the Midland and Southern, derivative of Anglo-Saxon *rād* (riding).

IV

Various words of more popular origin than these historic forms have from time to time passed from the dialects into Standard English. *Clever*, which was in

* *i.e.* " an enclosed or fortified place."

current use by the beginning of the Eighteenth Century, is probably a word of local East Anglian origin. *Fun*, first recorded in 1685, is a dialectal variation of another word now obsolete. The Nineteenth Century brought into general use several words which had previously belonged to a particular area. *Shunt*, which is known in early Middle English, had for centuries survived only as an obscure dialectal word, until the development of railways brought it into general currency about the middle of the Nineteenth Century, doubtless from its use by certain of the employees. A little later *trolley*, a local Suffolk word, entered the English vocabulary in the same way. The verb *scamp*, " to work negligently," is another word probably of dialectal origin which the Industrial Revolution added to the common stock. Certain words which are a puzzle to the etymologist are assumed on evidence of varying certainty to have passed from one of the dialects into general use. *Gamble* and *gambler*, which are not found until the middle of the Eighteenth Century, are thought to be dialectal survivals derived from a Middle English verb " gamenen," " to sport, or play." The noun *freak* is also perhaps dialectal, so too —as one might conjecture from its form—is the verb *flummox*. *Fluke*, which has been traced back to 1857, is perhaps identical with the local Whitby word *fluke*, " a guess." Probably most people instinctively recognize

in these and similar words the want of a distinguished
pedigree.

V

Curiosity about the remoter parts of the kingdom
has also been responsible for the introduction of
various dialect words into Standard English. Often
enough this curiosity has been inspired by literature.
Books of travel, " regional " poetry and fiction have
produced a sense that the manners and thoughts, the
climate and geography of remote districts are often
peculiar to themselves and cannot be fitly described
except in their own local terms. In the Fourteenth
Century the speakers of East Midland saw little need to
import words from other districts into their own : the
North and West of England were to them "uplandish,"
Scotland and Ireland were foreign and probably re-
pellent. But all this was gradually changed. As the
influence of the central government spread further
and further into the distant parts of the kingdom,
those parts came nearer and nearer to the thoughts and
imagination of London and its neighbourhood. Expressive local words in poems and books of travel
were repeated with relish, and many of these finally
secured a place in the English vocabulary.

The contribution of Scotland to Standard English is
fairly large. Both the Gaelic-speaking Highlands and

the English-speaking Lowlands have added various words to our vocabulary. The Scots dialect spoken in Southern Scotland was originally the same as that of Northern England, but by the Eighteenth Century it had come to possess a strongly-marked national character. A succession of gifted poets from the Fourteenth Century onward—Barbour, Douglas, Dunbar, Lindsay, and others—had given their language a fine literary tradition, and though Standard English more and more affected the language of educated people in Scotland, the dialect survived both in common memory and in the living speech of the humbler folk. The genius of Burns, whose best songs were in dialect, delighted the cultivated and patriotic critics of Edinburgh, and the enthusiasm soon spread to the South. Many of Burns's songs became familiar, and some of his characteristic words began to enter the ordinary language. The interest felt in England for the dialect of Scotland reached its height in the time of Scott, and it has since then been fostered by Carlyle, by Stevenson, and in our own time by Barrie and others. These writers have made Lowland Scots more or less familiar to thousands of English readers, and various words from the Scotch vocabulary have already passed into ordinary English; others may well do so in the future.

Among the earliest recorded words of the Lowland

dialect which have since become English are *wizened*
and *wraith*, both of which occur in Douglas's translation of the *Æneid* (1513). The same poem contains
the earliest known example of the Gaelic *slogan*. The
typical word *feud* (originally English) recrossed the
Border in the Sixteenth Century; *plaid* and *clan* are
occasionally used by English writers of the Seventeenth
Century. After the Union between the two countries,
the influx of Scotch words increased; the significant
term " Scotticism " is found in 1717. The lively interest felt in Scotch affairs in 1745, and the romantic curiosity which drove English travellers of the Eighteenth
Century into the Northern wilds brought more words
into use. *Loch* and *whisky* occur, with explanatory
notes, before 1750; *filibeg* (first recorded in an Act of
Parliament, 1746), *claymore* and *cairn* were familiar-
ised by Pennant and other English travellers. The
interest in the Lowland dialect stimulated by Burns
and Scott was a phase of the Romantic Movement, and
many Scotch words have become current through
their power of romantic suggestion. *Croon* and *eerie*
owe their vogue in part to Burns, and the phrase *lang
syne* has virtually become a part of the language in reminiscence of his well-known song. Scott's genius for
reviving old words was as fruitfully employed on
Middle and Elizabethan English as on Lowland Scots.
Many words which he recalled to life have not, indeed,

entered ordinary English, but his influence on the literary language has been equalled by no other writer of the last century.* Burns and Scott helped to create an English habit of borrowing Scotch words for their colour and associations ; many of the words so introduced are of an expressive and racy kind, *e.g.*, *rampage*, *fogey*, *outspoken*, *lilt*, the last-named being first recorded in Carlyle. Various Scotch words have been added to what one may call our " nursery vocabulary," *e.g.*, *cosy*, *bairn*, *wee*. *Pony* is another Scotch diminutive. The employment of Scotsmen in journalism is perhaps responsible for the recent vogue of such words as the verb *forgather* and the noun *forbear* (ancestor).

A Scotch *glen*, a Scotch *burn* are very different from an English dale and an English stream ; such dialectal words are therefore valuable additions to our vocabulary. Similarly, various local words from the remoter parts of England have entered into Standard English. This result, however, seems to be seldom produced except by the power of imaginative literature. For example, the Lakeland words *fell*, *beck*, *tarn* and *gill* (or *ghyll*), refer to very distinct features of the landscape to which there are no parallels in the East Midlands. But these words have become generally known, not because they are geographically indispensable, but

* See pages 202-204.

because they are common in the poems of Wordsworth and the other Lake Poets. Had Ireland and
Wales produced a novelist of the rank of Scott those
lands would have had a much greater influence on the
English language; as it is their contributions to its
vocabulary are comparatively small. A few words of
Irish Gaelic have entered the English language, *e.g.*,
bog, *brogue*, *galore* (literally " to sufficiency "), *sham-
rock*, *tory*; in more recent times political movements
have given currency to *Fenian* and *Sinn Feinn*.
Equally small is the contribution of Welsh. A possible
early borrowing is *flannel*; *cromlech* belongs to the
Seventeenth Century, *eisteddfod* is more recent, and
there are a few others. The Dominions and the
United States will no doubt in the future add many
new words to the English vocabulary, and the welfare
of the language will depend partly on the quality of
their contribution.

CHAPTER V
POETIC WORDS

MANY languages are the expression of national character. This is especially true of those which have
begun in an unformed state and have been gradually
moulded by history, by literature, by the consciousness of the people. The English nation and the
English language resemble each other in their mixed
origin, and time has produced in them a similarity
of soul. Such at least is the testimony of foreign
observers who, on this subject, are probably the best.
The characteristics of the English people as shown in
history are energy, love of freedom, and a sense of the
practical. The description which the Danish philologist, Jespersen, gives of the English language
uses almost identical terms. " A methodical, energetic business-like and sober language that does
not care much for finery and elegance, but does
care for logical consistency and is opposed to any
attempt to narrow-in life by police regulations and
strict rules either of grammar or of lexicon. As the
language is, so also is the nation."

Of the epithets in this quotation, " methodical,"

" business-like," " sober," and " logical " are in a class by themselves and refer to the practical and prosaic merits of language. Love of liberty and energy which Jespersen also attributes to English are qualities of a different kind. They refer to the nature of the language in its more creative aspect; in the deepest sense of the word, to its poetry. All languages must contain the elements of both law and liberty : by law they are faithful to their own past and continue to be intelligible ; by liberty they are saved from dull uniformity, and give some scope to individual expression. But though both elements are necessary, they need not exist in the same proportion. It has been the boast of some languages that their words are clear and precise in meaning, free from ambiguity, and of an ascertained and admitted significance. Such, in general, is the character of languages which have submitted to the authority of an Academy ; it is true of the Romance languages in general, and of French— especially French in the Classical age—in particular. The characteristic of English, on the other hand, has been its freedom. The boldness of Shakespeare and the other Elizabethans as makers of language is a much more significant phenomenon than the authority wielded by Dr. Johnson ; the creative spirit of the one is in harmony with the inmost character of the English language, while the other's love of rigid definition and his dislike of " low " and inelegant language, though valuable in their day, were the expression of a half-foreign classicism, not, like the intensely native and natural style of Shakespeare, " for all time." The style, and in some measure the vocabulary, of almost every great English poet from Spenser onwards has been highly individual. Many of our own poets have been among our most successful word-makers ; and even those who have not added new words to the dictionary have given new suggestions, new associations, to words already existing. This could never have been done had not the genius of the language made it possible ; for language makes the poet, no less than the poet makes the language. " We must be free or die, who speak the tongue That Shakespeare spake " is an utterance which links together the nation and the language with profound insight. Energy, likewise, is an enduring quality of our vocabulary. The term " energy " is itself borrowed from the language of criticism, and properly means " expressiveness." We have already seen the power of English to create expressive words, and to give old words a more expressive form. These, indeed, are the most useful achievements of the popular talent for word-creation. In making words more nobly and more intensely expressive, poetry merely brings out the latent qualities of the language and completes its unfulfilled destiny.

The praise bestowed by Gray on Shakespeare, " every word in him is a picture," is peculiarly appropriate to the greatest of English poets. But as the greatest master of our language, Shakespeare illustrates, by his practice, the essential qualities of that language. In poetry our vocabulary appears in its most character-istic aspect.

I

In the language of our greatest poets, freedom and energy are both present. They are individual in their choice of words, and their use of them is intensely expressive : the two phases of their art, indeed, are complementary. In several of our poets, however, there is more freedom than energy, as in others there is more energy than freedom. Generally speaking, we find the quality of freedom in epic, narrative, and descriptive verse, the quality of energy in drama. Again, freedom is typical of Elizabethan and " Roman-tic," energy of " Classical " poetry. But, as we have said, the greatest styles unite both qualities.

No English poet was ever more free in his choice of words than Edmund Spenser. His position in time as the first of the great Elizabethan poets gave him a com-manding influence. Had Spenser's language been as expressive as it was original, he would have been one of the greatest word-makers of our literature. But many of Spenser's words live only in his own poems, or in the pages of those who have affected a Spenserian style. Ben Jonson's remark that he " writ no language " justly indicates the qualified measure of his success. None the less, Spenser's works are still alive, and we understand his words though we do not adopt them. The widespread fame of *The Faerie Queene* has indeed resulted in introducing two or three Spenserian words into common speech, *e.g.*, *blatant*, *braggadocio*. These, however, are from names of characters in the poem ; like *Quixotic* and *Malapropism*, they are a testimony to literary power, not to skill in word-making.

The chief feature of Spenser's poetic vocabulary is the diversity of the sources from which it is drawn. Just as *The Faerie Queene* is an unworldly poem, based on legend, romance, and its author's own far-ranging dreams, so his language is also unworldly, being drawn not from the idiom of his own day but from the vocabulary of Chaucer, and Malory, and of other old writers. To some extent, also, he borrows from the rustic dialects, though not so much as in *The Shepherd's Calendar*. *Als*, *ne*, *whilom*, *eke*, *whylere*—such words as these, already obsolete, or soon to become so, are scattered broadcast over his pages. He loves poetic variations : a knight is sometimes an *elf*, sometimes a *wight*, sometimes a *faery's son*. He uses many new compound-verbs, such as *outshine* and *over-*

awe. Various privative adjectives such as *weetless* and *woundless* are first found in his poems. French words flavoured with romantic memories, such as *belamour* and *emprise*, give colour to his style ; indeed zeal for " atmosphere " sometimes betrays him into inaccuracy, as in his misuse of *chevisaunce* for " riding "—an error copied by many of his followers. *Empurple* is a characteristic Spenserian verb. Words drawn direct from Latin and often used in their etymological sense find place in his vocabulary : *daedal* (an echo of " dædala tellus ") *liquid* in the sense of " clear, transparent," *lucid* in the sense of " shining." The *oread* enters his verse from classical mythology, as well as many stranger beings such as the *scolopendra*. He loves the double epithet such as *sea-shouldering*, a word applied to the whale, and *rosy-fingered*, the equivalent of Homer's epithet for the dawn. Words good and bad, true and false, mingle in his verse. Among many which are rich in colour and beautiful sound, we find some which are awkwardly formed and ineffective, *e.g.*, *addoom*, *admirance*, *adviceful*, as well as false archaisms like *ygo* for " ago." Spenser's work is the best illustration of Gray's remark that a poet's language is never that of his age.

Spenser's influence on our poetry has been very great. We are told by Dryden that Milton acknowledged Spenser as his model. Poets so different as

Cowley and Keats were enchanted by him in their boyhood, and indeed he seems to have had a unique power of awakening latent poetical talent to a first consciousness of itself. Spenser is, in fact, the founder of our Poetic Diction. His world of words is not only more beautiful but more free and expansive than the English of any one age. His archaisms, his wealth of synonyms, his dialectal words, his compound words, his reminiscences of romantic and classical writers have directly or indirectly influenced the language of almost all the epic, narrative, and descriptive poets who have succeeded him. Since Spenser, poetry and poetic prose have become the last refuge of many words which have disappeared from our ordinary vocabulary. Thus, for the one word " sea " we have the poetic words *main*, *deep* and *surge*. Hundreds of archaic or unusual words and forms which would startle us in everyday speech seem perfectly natural in poetry, from the sounded *-ed* of the past tense and past participle or the familiar form *morn* for " morning " to rarer words such as Tennyson's *marish* for " marsh," Keats's *leafits* for " leaflets," or Milton's *drear* for " dreary." Spenser's *empurple* is paralleled by Milton's *embrown*, *ensanguined*, and many similar formations in other poets. Quite in the Spenserian manner is the adverb *agape* first found in *Paradise Lost*. On the analogy of this or some similar word, an extraordinary number of poetic adverbs appeared in Nineteenth Century verse : *adangle* and *aflicker* in Browning ; *achill* in Morris ; *aflower* in Swinburne ; *aflush* in Hopkins ; and in others, *agleam*, *aglint*, *aglimmer*. Reminiscences of classical mythology are not peculiarly Spenserian ; but it is noteworthy that since Spenser's time Poetic Diction has been accumulating more and more decorative words from classical poetry, *e.g.*, Milton's *amaranthine* and *ambrosial*. Milton followed Spenser in increasing the distance between prose and poetry by using various words in their etymological rather than their current sense : *error*, for instance, of the wandering course of rivers :

> With mazie *error* under pendant shades ;
> (*Paradise Lost*, iv. 239.)

lapse, of the gliding of water :

> Liquid *lapse* of murmuring streams ;
> (*Paradise Lost*, viii. 263.)

explode, in the sense of " hiss off the stage " :

> Him old and young
> *Exploded*, and had seized with violent hands.
> (*Paradise Lost*, xi. 664-5.)

Since Spenser's time, too, the compound word, especially the compound epithet, has become one of the most distinctive features of poetic language. Gray's *ivy-mantled* tower, Keats's *far-foamed* sands, *deep-damask'd* wings, *chain-droop'd* lamp, Tennyson's *dewy-tassell'd* wood, show how rich in pictorial power words of this type may be. Even the weaker qualities of Spenser's diction are paralleled in subsequent poets. The extreme liberty of his vocabulary has a counterpart in the recklessness which sometimes disfigures the language of so great a poet as Browning. Such a formation, for instance, as Browning's pseudo-archaic *gadge*, to denominate an imaginary instrument of torture, comes near to violating the first principle of language, that it should convey a meaning. But any good quality may be abused, and the gain to poetry from Spenser's example has, on a wide survey, been immense. A vocabulary of ample extent, not circumscribed by time or literary fashion, has been kept open for the poet; and in this freedom the poet has been able to keep what for him is the " eternal jewel "—his individuality.

II

Spenser's style illustrates the value of liberty in expression; Shakespeare's the supreme virtue of energy. Spenser has often been called " the poet's poet," and his great influence on the language of poetry is one justification for the title. Shakespeare is the poet for all men, and his influence extends to the whole language. His words and his example have penetrated far into the common English which is our general heritage. Both poets were the sons of a great age; both spoke a language which was in the freshness of its youth and still uncorrupted. The freedom of the time which encouraged experiments in expression, not insisting on the parts of speech, but allowing noun, verb and adjective to exchange their several functions, gave them an opportunity which has never since recurred. Just as all English poets have inherited some part of the Elizabethan spirit through Spenser, so all to whom English is their native tongue have inherited something of the same spirit through Shakespeare and the Authorized Version of the Bible.

On the surface, the most striking feature of Shakespeare's vocabulary is its amplitude. A Concordance of his works contains about 23,000 words, more than three times the number used by Milton. That so large a quantity of Elizabethan and Jacobean English should be kept alive by the vitality of Shakespeare's genius is a matter of obvious significance to the language. The Authorized Version of the Bible is also a vast repository of bygone English; but the vocabulary of the Bible is a conglomerate from various periods, and many of its words and phrases are a deposit from speech much older than that of Elizabeth's age. Shakespeare's language was the newest language of his time. His object was intense energy of expression. He never used antique words in the manner of Spenser. If he used dialect it was for a dramatic purpose, as in the disguised language with which Edgar misleads Oswald in *King Lear*.* A full list of the common words first recorded in Shakespeare's works would give an impressive illustration of his "modernity." Here are a few: *air* in the sense of (*a*) "aspect," (*b*) "melody"; *action*, in the sense of "fight"; *amazing, dauntless, defeat* (as substantive), *dishearten, enrapt, far-off, footfall, fretful, laughable, look forward, sick* ("thoroughly wearied"), *stand* ("undergo," also "endure without flinching"), *duteous, dwindle, domineer.* It is too much to assume that these words were coined by Shakespeare, though some at least probably were. In any case, a man who helped to introduce so many useful words into the language must be reckoned among its benefactors. Not that all Shakespeare's "new" words are well formed or necessary. Some have been rarely or never used since his time. A few are badly coined, *e.g., reverb*, from "reverbero," which has been replaced by the more regular "reverberate." *Attask* from the verb "to task" is an unfortunate "nonce-word" for "take to task"; *subduement* is not too harshly dismissed by Dr. Johnson as "a word not used, nor worthy to be used." In fact, as we know so well, Shakespeare was a great poet but only a moderate scholar. Subsequent genera-

* Act IV, Scene vi.

tions have rejected a few of his words as ill-made and needless—the natural progress of the language has discarded certain others ; but when every deduction is made, it is wonderful how little of his vocabulary has become obsolete. He dealt with matters permanently interesting to men, with an intensity of expression which could not be surpassed.

The freedom with which the parts of speech were altered in Elizabethan English is well described by Dr. Abbott in his *Shakespearian Grammar*. "You can *happy* your friend, *malice* or *foot* your enemy, or *fall* an axe on his neck." It is fortunate for the ordinary purposes of language that this extreme liberty has been long since renounced ; the landmarks of grammar are now more firmly fixed. But in poetry this Elizabethan prerogative was often used with great effect. Innumerable passages in Shakespeare owe part of their force to words made new and arresting by this means. A few examples will illustrate this. In Hamlet's famous soliloquy the adjective " sickly " is transformed into a verb :

Sicklied o'er with the pale cast of thought.
(Act III, Sc. i.)

By similar means a new verb is added to the language in Macbeth's outcry :

No ; this my hand will rather
The multitudinous seas *incarnadine*.
(Act II, Sc. ii.)

The extraordinary vividness of language in *Antony and Cleopatra* owes much to the same device :

> For her own person,
> It *beggar'd* all description ;
>
> > (Act ii, Sc. ii.)
>
> He *words* me, girls, he *words* me ;
>
> > (Act v, Sc. ii.)
>
> > A hand that kings
> Have *lipp'd*, and trembled kissing.
>
> > (Act ii, Sc. v.)

" *Spurn* " as a noun ; " *dialogue*," " *sermon*," " *fang*," " *example*," as verbs are instances chosen at random from *Timon of Athens* ; and from any of the other plays, especially those written after 1600, a considerable list might be drawn. The parts of speech are still altered at times by poets with something of the Elizabethan freedom. That the tradition has survived is certainly due in large measure to the example of Shakespeare. Keats, who was a close student of Shakespeare's language, has used the device very much in the spirit of his master, as when he transforms " monitor " * into a verb ; and again when he changes an intransitive into a transitive verb in his *Ode to Psyche* :

> Leaves and *trembled* blossoms, where there ran
> A brooklet, scarce espied.

" Globed peonies "—a phrase of the same poet—shows

* *Endymion,* iv. 884.

how the device is an aid to vivid metaphor ; so does Shelley's " islanded," in :

> Beneath is spread like a green sea
> The waveless plain of Lombardy,
> Bounded by the vaporous air,
> *Islanded* by cities fair ; *

or Arnold's " bower " in :

> And *bower* me from the August sun with shade.†

Every reader of English poetry knows that this combination of freedom and expressiveness in the use of words is one of its winning qualities.

Shakespeare's language is vitally metaphorical. No English poet—perhaps no poet in any literature—can approach him in the force and abundance of his figurative expressions. When Othello has occasion to say that an old campaigner can dispense with luxury he does it in these words :

> The tyrant custom, most grave senators,
> Hath made the flinty and steel couch of war
> My thrice-driven bed of down.
>
> (Act I, Sc. iii.)

Nothing could surpass the energy of the contrast between the two metaphors " flinty " and " steel " on the one hand, and the " bed of down " made trebly soft by a newly-coined epithet on the other. Such expressions

---

* *The Euganean Hills*, 90-94.
† *The Scholar Gipsy*, 29.

are not exceptional in Shakespeare : they are characteristic of half his work. Good metaphors are always apt to be repeated, and Shakespeare is constantly enriching the language through the memory of his readers. Macbeth's utterance (Act v, Sc. iii) :

> My way of life
> Is fallen into the sere, the yellow leaf,

has added a familiar phrase to the language, and many other metaphors, such as Cleopatra's " salad days " and Hamlet's " caviare to the general," have become almost as common. Some of the most familiar figures of speech, *e.g.*, *sleep*, in the sense of " rest peacefully," as of sunlight on a bank ; *silken*, in the sense of " effeminate " ; *fire*, in the sense of " illumine," as of the rising sun behind trees ; and even *snail* in the sense of " sluggard," are first recorded in Shakespeare ; and it seems certain that some at least of these expressions are his inventions. He was fond, too, of transferring words from one set of associations to another. Needing an adverb to add great depth of feeling to the action of " wishing " he borrows it from religion and thus gives the word " devoutly " a new sense :

> 'tis a consummation
> *Devoutly* to be wished.
>
> (*Hamlet*, Act III, Sc. i.)

Lecture, in the sense of admonitory speech, is

first found in Shakespeare; so also is *sanctimonious* (originally " holy "), in its current sense " holy in outward profession." A single word may, in Shakespeare's hands, be used to convey many new shades of meaning : for example, *gild* may mean " bribe with gold " (" offence's *gilded* hand "), or " smear " (" I'll *gild* the faces of the grooms withal ") or " transfigure with sunlight " (" *gilding* pale streams with heavenly alchemy "). Such " generalization " is of the very essence of Shakespeare's style. Vast as was his vocabulary, it was not large enough for all the thoughts and images he had to convey. He stretched the capacities of the language almost to breaking-point, but he permanently increased its range of expression.

Like most writers who breathed the air of the Renaissance, Shakespeare helped to introduce many new words from Latin. Some of his coinages are valuable additions to the language, *e.g.*, *multitudinous* from " multitudo," first found in the great passage from *Macbeth* already quoted. *Deracinate* is first recorded in *Henry V*, and is used again in a line of great vigour in *Troilus and Cressida* :

Divert and crack, rend and deracinate.

The number of felicitous phrases and expressions which have entered the language from the plays of the "middle period" is almost past reckoning. From *Hamlet* come: "more honoured in the breach than the observance," "cudgel thy brains," "out-herods Herod," "suit the action to the word," "towering passion," "yeoman's service," "witching time of night," and many more. From *Othello* come "seamy side," "melting mood," "puny whipster," "foregone conclusion," "pride, pomp, and circumstance." "Time-honoured" is from *Richard II*, "lack-lustre" from *As You Like It*, "spirit-stirring" from *Othello*. "Be-all and end-all" is from *Macbeth*, so are "coign of vantage" and "make assurance doubly sure"; * and *fitful* is a word which has entered the language from a phrase in the same play, "life's fitful fever." Shakespeare's plays are among the most popular works in literature; but it is not only the popularity of the plays and the familiarity of their language that have given their author so vast an influence on our vocabulary: it is the inherent excellence of his language, its picturesque force, its graphic energy. Shakespeare is the supreme example of the poetic word-maker.

III

No other English poet has possessed the equal of Shakespeare's magic in calling new words into being. But all great and original poetry influences the language

* "Double sure," in the original; IV. i. 83.

in which it is written, and is likely, in proportion to its
extent, to enrich it with words and phrases. A writer
so powerful as Milton has naturally left an impress on
the tongue ; but his influence is widely different from
that of Shakespeare. Milton's style, unlike Shakespeare's, has strongly-marked features which tempt
imitation, and for a century English verse was strewn
with such phrases as " the finny drove " and " the
meadow's fleecy store," by writers who supposed
these to be the epic equivalents of " fish " and
" sheep." But Milton's permanent additions to our
vocabulary are comparatively few. In his early poems
he retained something of the Elizabethan freedom of
word-formation ; but in the epics and the tragedy of
his old age, he chose his words with a strictness not
less marked than the complexity of his syntax and the
infinite variety of his verse. His chief fault is a tendency towards Latinism ; to use *denounce* in the sense of
" announce " after " denuntiare," or to coin a word like
debel from " debellare " is quite in keeping with his
manner. His vocabulary is much smaller than Shakespeare's, but it is also more monumental and more
scholarly. He chose such words as were likely to endure, and they have endured. The speeches which open
Book II of *Paradise Lost* have been justly cited as the
most perfect examples of the classical style in English.
But the whole of Milton's vocabulary in his later poems

has this quality : it is classical in its clearness, its strength, its restraint.

The style of Milton's early poems can scarcely be overpraised. They have the " Doric delicacy " which pleased Sir Henry Wotton, as well as the compressed phrasing which delighted Macaulay. It is natural that many of the felicitous expressions in these charming pieces should have been so often repeated that they have become a part of the language. The epithet *chequered* in the special sense which it bears in *L'Allegro* :

> Dancing in the *chequer'd* shade,

has been adopted into the language of description. " Quips and cranks " is a phrase which has been borrowed from the same poem, and from *Il Penseroso* comes the word *fleecy*, used as an epithet for sky or cloud. *Freaked*, a word formed by Milton in *Lycidas* meaning " streaked," has been adopted by various poets, though it has never become common. From *Comus* come the epithet *love-lorn*, there applied to the nightingale, and the phrase " silver lining " describing the inner side of a cloud. *Wassailer*, a new formation from " wassail," occurs in the same poem and has been used by Coleridge and other writers.

That *Paradise Lost* could be written at all is a high testimony to the wealth of our vocabulary in the Seventeenth Century. The vast scheme of the poet compelled him to create a certain number of new words, but these instead of encumbering the language have greatly added to its wealth. It is possible that the noun *gloom*, which occurs in *Paradise Lost*, and elsewhere in the poet's works, is the creation of Milton, being derived, apparently, by back-formation from " gloomy." Besides this there are certain words created to embody the poet's conceptions of vast space, such as *dimensionless* and *infinitude*. *Anarch* comes from the description of Chaos as " the anarch old." *Archangelic* and *archfiend* are Miltonic words, so also is *Satanic*, which has replaced the older " Satanical." *Pandemonium*, the name of the palace built by Mulciber for the infernal host, has become an English word, and several descriptive terms such as *emblazonry* have been often repeated. Many Miltonic phrases, such as " darkness visible," from the description of Hell ; " pillar of state," from the portrait of Beelzebub as he rises to address the " infernal peers " ; " bad eminence," of Satan's exalted position in Pandemonium, have become part of the language. The fulness of Milton's wordmaking power cannot be measured apart from his prose-works ; but the creations of his verse have been more enduring, for whereas mere erudition is often uppermost in his pamphlets, art is always predominant in his poetry.

IV

Spenser, Milton and Shakespeare are the three greatest of our poetic word-makers. The first two, for purposes of their own, widened the gap between prose and poetry; the third enlarged the scope of human expression by means which were possible in his own day, and possible only then. When the great changes of 1660 gave a wholly new turn to English life and thought, poetry descended from the heights to dwell for a while in the realm of political warfare and social criticism. In the hands of Dryden, the English language lost the divine audacity of its greatest days and became a sober, forcible instrument for controversy and satire. Many approved of the change, and Dr. Johnson, in the next century, applying to Dryden the praise bestowed on the re-builder of Rome, declared that he had found our language brick and left it marble. Dryden added some useful words to the vocabulary of criticism, but in his verse he aimed chiefly at directness and sobriety, though, as Gray has shown, the diction of his poetry is still widely different from that of prose. The poets of the Eighteenth Century, following Dryden's lead, added few new words to our language. Some imitated the manner of Milton, some of Spenser, some pursued the plainer path marked out by Dryden and Pope: few aspired to be originators. The contribution of poetry to our vocabulary for a hundred years or so after 1660 is extremely small. Onomatopoeic words, one or two, may perhaps have been added, such as *coo*, first recorded in a drama of Dryden's; also a few compounds, such as *day-dream*, another of Dryden's formations, and *snow-flake*, first found in a poem of 1734 called *Cupid and Psyche*. The literary reputation of Pope was enormous, but his poetic ideal of " correctness " prevented him from making many new words. *Fateful* and *funereal* are adjectives first recorded in his translations of Homer, and *casuistry* is one of the few memorials in our language of his genius for satire. The creative spirit of the Eighteenth Century was more active in its prose than its verse.

The poets of the Romantic Movement opened new regions of imagination and feeling. Once more the spirit of daring and adventure entered into the English language. But great as were the poets of the new age, it was impossible that they should set so deep a mark on our vocabulary as their predecessors of the Seventeenth Century. The work of critic and lexicographer had not been done in vain. It is true that Johnson in the Preface to his *Dictionary* denies that he can " fix our language, and put a stop to those alterations which time and chance have hitherto been suffered to make in it without opposition." Yet Johnson's influence and the spirit of the age did something towards producing this result. English could never again be passive material for poetic genius to mould and transform at will, any more than it could be the helpless prey of ignorant caprice or learned eccentricity. Nor had the Romantic poets themselves much desire for wild innovation in language. They sought rather to put into currency a richer store of words, to restore the simplicity and the glamour of that older English which the age of politeness had set aside as antiquated. Wordsworth, who stated in a preface to his poems that there could be " no essential difference " between the language of prose and metrical composition, rarely created a new word ; and except for the spelling *ghyll* of the dialectal " gill," and one or two modest formations such as *treeless*, which he perhaps originated, he has added nothing new to the vocabulary. Coleridge has contributed many words to philosophy, but in his poetry he restored rather than created ; one of his revivals is *jargoning* for the song of birds, which he borrowed from Chaucer. Byron introduced, or helped to give currency to many words from the Levant ; and his use of outlandish terms such as *ataghan* (a sword of Mohammedan countries), *caïque* (a skiff used on the Bosporus), *giaour* (a Turkish name of reproach for a Christian), *jereed* (a wooden javelin), *palampore* (a bed-cover), *tophaike* (a musket), caused a delightful thrill in many a quiet English home. No poet of the age possessed such a talent for word-making as Keats : in this respect he is—to use Arnold's phrase—" with Shakespeare." Many of his finest formations, however, are the lovely compound epithets for which there is no fit use out of their own context. In transferring the parts of speech he had something of Shakespeare's boldness, but such expressions as *loamed* for " stained with loam," and *foamed along* for the career of a chariot drawn by foaming horses, are " nonce-words " not likely to be repeated. But the felicity of some of his words has been too great to be resisted. *Wailful,* * an epithet from the *Ode to Autumn* (" Then in a wailful choir the small gnats mourn "), has been borrowed by Bridges and Meredith, *serpentry* from *Endymion* by Ruskin and Browning, *realmless* from *Hyperion* by Lowell and Lytton. The earliest record of *envisage* is in *Hyperion*, and it is possible that Keats was the first to adopt from French this now somewhat hackneyed word. In revealing a new wealth of sensuous beauty in the English language Keats has been one of the greatest influences on modern literary style. Perhaps the most characteristic mark left on our vocabulary by the Romantic Movement has been the addition of new words to suggest a certain imaginative outlook. The adjective

* Not invented by Keats, but apparently first used by him in this sense.

eerie, used by Burns in 1792, was quickly adopted
by writers of Romantic verse and prose. *Quaint,* in its
now usual sense, became current about the same time.
Weird was originally a noun meaning " fate," and
Shakespeare's phrase " the weird sisters " means " the
witches." But in the poems of Shelley *weird* is used as
an adjective in the sense of "uncanny"; and so popular did this new Romantic word become that it soon
produced derivatives such as *weirdness, weirdly* and
weird-like.

In diction the Victorian poets were less original
than their predecessors. They chose rather to benefit
from the accumulated experience of the past. Tennyson, the greatest artist among them, was above all
things an eclectic. A supreme master of the language,
his respect for its traditions was so great that he
avoided experiments of the bolder kind. He revived
and he coined various words, and though his formations
are not dynamic, they are invariably skilful and often
picturesque. His ruling passion for the sea is revealed
in the large number of compound words he formed of
which *sea-* is the first element, *e.g., sea-haze, sea-dunes,
sea-graves, sea-blue, sea-smoke.* A few archaic words
such as *gride* are revived in his verse, and he has coined
at least one onomatopoeia, the noun *lin-lan-lone,* in a
description of bells, in a late poem. Of Tennyson's
contemporaries, Browning was the boldest experi-

menter in language. His genius, however, lay rather in extending the bounds of poetry than in giving new beauty and expression to words. His vocabulary is vast, but it is the vocabulary of living passion, of philosophical analysis, rather than of pure poetry. New words occur in his verse, but many are such as the language has no need of, such as the strange *encolure* for the mane of a horse. If, however, he is the inventor of *artistry*, of which the first known instance occurs in *The Ring and the Book*, at least one good word stands to his credit. Victorian poetry, however, is still recent, and it is too early to assess its contribution to the language. Still less can we forecast the influence of Bridges, Doughty and others who in our century have experimented in poetic diction.

CHAPTER VI
COMPOSITION AND DERIVATION

EVERY civilized language must possess the means of its own growth. Knowledge, thought and experience are always expanding and, though few people give the matter much thought, there is no need to doubt that the English language will prove equal to the fresh demands which the future may make upon it. For centuries English has been a borrowing language, and thanks to its power of naturalization, it has successfully assimilated thousands of foreign words. But the power of " making " words is as important as the power of borrowing them. A language must be able to increase itself from its own resources. Of the various methods by which the English vocabulary is enlarged, none is more important than the process of joining two or more words together to form a new one. Many words in the earliest known writings of the language are formed by composition, and many new compounds were formed during the Anglo-Saxon period. The methods of word-composition have somewhat changed since the earliest times, and they have also been widely extended. Fresh compounds are formed continually, and though some perish almost as soon as they are created, others, through their usefulness or their aptness, have survived for centuries. Words may unite to serve some transient need, or they may remain inseparably knit.

I. Nouns and Adjectives

Compounds are most simply formed when a pair or group of words frequently used together in a normal grammatical relation are regarded or written as a single word. Thus the noun *daisy* consisted, in its earliest form, of *daeges* and *eage* (day's eye). The composition was merely the welding together of a phrase into a word. The noun *blackbird* is of a similar kind. The accentuation reveals the difference between a compound and a pair of words ; for the pronunciation of *blackbird* differs from that of " black bird." In certain compounds of the kind, however, *e.g.*, *matter-of-fact*, the separate elements retain their full accentuation, and the composition consists in no more than hyphening or connecting the parts of a phrase.

Formal composition of this kind has played a comparatively small part in the making of English. In the majority of compounds, the normal grammatical function of one of the elements is changed. As the principles which govern composition are very lax, the process has been freely, perhaps too freely, used. One of the simplest and oldest ways of forming a compound is to place one noun in an attributive relation with another. This method has been used throughout the history of the language. Thus, when someone wished to express the concept " horizon," he did so by forming the compound *sea-rim*. There is no limit to the number of such formations possible, though many serve only a temporary use. When a compound becomes permanently fixed, the hyphen is usually dropped, especially when the original sense is modified, as in *cupboard*. Many compounds have become familiar nouns in common use, *e.g.*, *rainbow*, *earthquake*, *hailstone*, and it is difficult to imagine the time when such words did not exist. But the peculiar function of composition is to fill some gap in the vocabulary revealed by a particular or temporary need; though naturally some such compounds will survive the occasion which created them. For example, the noun *storm* was for centuries sufficiently precise for the ordinary needs of expression; but towards the end of the Sixteenth Century it was found convenient to form the compound *hail-storm*, which was followed about a hundred years later by *snow-storm*; and it is significant that these two words, in which a hyphen is still commonly employed, are both more recent by centuries than the three examples just quoted. The right of forming compound nouns at will is a great advantage to poets who can give a new aspect to familiar things by such words as *day-star*. So, too, the translator who can find no single word to serve his purpose will often have recourse to a compound, as Tindale did in *mercy-seat*. Compounds are often formed deliberately as " nonce-words," and certain kinds of writing intended merely to arrest or startle, *e.g.*, advertisements, would be greatly impoverished if deprived of this old and useful method of word-formation.

The great part played by Composition in English is due to two main causes, both of which have made it a convenient rather than a precise method of word-formation. In the first place, the relation between the elements need not be fully expressed and can be interpreted by the sense. Thus, a *rocking-horse* is a horse which rocks, but a *dining-room* is not a room which dines. Secondly, the licence of modifying the parts of speech in certain ways for the purpose of neatness or compression has produced such compounds as *deep-dyed* and *treble-sinewed*, in which " deep " fulfils the function of an adverb, and " sinewed " is a quasi-participle formed from a noun. Though compounds were freely created during the earlier periods of the language, the practice reached its culmination in the late Sixteenth and early Seventeenth Centuries. Fortunately, however, the best writers of those years used their freedom in the service of graphic or forcible expression, and many of their compounds, though perhaps intended as " nonce-words," have entered the ordinary vocabulary. For instance, *open-handed* and *open-hearted* (both of which are " parasynthetic " compounds formed from the phrases " open hand " and " open heart ") belong to the early Seventeenth Century, and roughly contemporary are *single-minded* and *close-fisted*, as well as the Shakespearian *foul-mouthed* and *open-eyed*. This type of compound is now regarded as perfectly regular, and many analogous examples have since been formed. Another regular though less common type is that in which the relation between the two elements is similar to the Latin construction, " accusative of respect," as in *headstrong*, *foot-sore*. So, too, we find verb combined with noun, as in *kill-joy* and *spendthrift*. In poetry, compounds are often formed without much regard for grammatical analogy, and such expressions as Shakespeare's " *steep-down* gulfs " or Keats's " *far-foamed* sands " must be judged simply by the standard of expressiveness.

Compounds are on the whole a somewhat informal class of words, and for that very reason they have long been dear to the English people. Our vocabulary contains many popular formations such as *claptrap*, *helter-skelter*, *hurly-burly*, *topsy-turvy*, which are generally reserved for informal occasions. Equally informal and equally expressive are such compounds as *happy-go-lucky*, *devil-may-care*. But English is also a language which profits much from wholesome discipline, and Dr. Johnson was probably performing a good service when he branded the compound *uncome-at-able* as "a low, corrupt word."

II. VERBS

New verbs have been formed in English by composition since quite early times, and the method was used during the Anglo-Saxon period. For example, the verb *let in* is found about the year A.D. 1000, and *let down* occurs about the middle of the Twelfth Century. The system has been extremely prolific, and many common verbs, *e.g.*, *give*, *set*, *take*, have, in composition with various adverbs, added scores of verbal phrases to the language. Further, the sense of certain adverbs is often subtly varied according to the verbs with which they are combined. Thus, in each of the phrases *serve out*, *hang out*, *put out*, *make out*, *fit out*, *call out*, the second element bears a slightly different sense. The system is also extremely elastic. In the earlier stages of the language these verbal phrases sometimes coalesced with single words, as in *doff* (do off), *don* (do on), and the Elizabethan *dout* (do out). In more recent times, verb and adverb have been generally written separately, as if to signify that the elements may be joined and parted at will. Numerous as are the verbal phrases, they are too few for all the purposes required by popular usage, and many compounds have to do duty for various meanings. Thus, *let off* has at least three senses : a landlord may let off a house, a soldier may let off a gun, a schoolmaster may let off a boy. But this is nothing to the variety of *set up*, which has in all—obsolete and dialectal usage being counted—some sixty different senses. This multiplication of meanings and the consequent danger of ambiguity are the chief objection to verbs of this kind. Some are needlessly overtasked. There is no reason, for instance, why *turn down* should be used in the slang sense of " reject," when it has already a both natural and useful meaning attached to it. The great vogue of these verbal phrases is due partly to a reaction against formality in language, and partly to their power of stimulating attention when made or manipulated by the skilled journalist. A good stylist avoids using them to the exclusion of other verbs, and will sometimes prefer the formal *admit* to the colloquial " let in." It is noteworthy that when the adverb precedes the verb in the phrase the effect is less informal, and poets have long preferred to form compounds after the manner used by the Authorized Version in such a sentence as

" Thou knowest my *downsitting* and my *uprising*."
The verb *outflew*, for example, in *Paradise Lost* : *

> He spake : and to confirm his words, *outflew*
> Millions of flaming swords,

is certainly more in harmony with the style than " flew
out," and there are many similar compound verbs,
e.g., *downcast*, *outpour*, which are now used only in
poetry.

III

In common with Latin and Greek, Anglo-Saxon
possessed the means of forming new words by means
of affixes. The suffix *-ness*, for example, by which we
now form an abstract noun from an adjective, exactly
corresponds in function to its origin, the *-nes* of Anglo-
Saxon. Some affixes, indeed, are so indispensable
that the language could scarcely have survived without
them. The affixes at present in use, however, have
been derived from various sources—from French,
from Latin and from Greek, as well as from Anglo-
Saxon. The fusion of the early French loan-words
with the native vocabulary was so complete that
certain of the French affixes obtained an independent
life and were attached to English words. Thus the
suffix *-ment* was originally French, yet it has been

* I, 663, 4.

frequently affixed to native words, as in *acknowledgement*, *betterment*, *wonderment*. Later, certain Latin and Greek affixes obtained the same sort of formative power, and were used not only in combination with Latin and Greek roots, but with various words current in English regardless of their origin. For instance, in *dishearten*, a Latin prefix has been attached to a purely native verb ; in *anti-Jacobin*, a Greek prefix has been attached to a noun borrowed from French. The question naturally arises, Can any affix be combined with any word, irrespective of the origin of both ?

Unfortunately no general answer is possible. In the past, the question was often not regarded etymologically, and at some periods the dislike of " hybrid " compounds is stronger than at others. Sometimes the matter has been decided by the relative vitality of rival affixes. There was, for example, in Middle English a struggle between the native *again-* and the Latin *re-* ; but whereas all such compounds as *again-buy* for " redeem," and *again-turn* for " return " are obsolete, the Latin prefix was more and more extensively used, and though first employed chiefly with words of Latin origin, was later freely prefixed to native verbs ; nor can it be denied that the more convenient prefix has triumphed. The number of verbs such as *remake*, *rename*, *reopen* now current, is beyond computation. Similarly, the useful suffix *-able*, though originally found only in words of French origin, was later extended to native words, as in *lovable*, *bearable*, *unshakable*. On the other hand the native *un-* was at one time strong enough to encroach on what would seem to be the province of the Latin *in-*, and during the Seventeenth Century many negative compounds were current, such as *unaccessible*, *unaccurate*, *unadequate*, *uncessant*, which now strike us as " hybrids." *Un-* is still an active prefix, but it is now not generally combined with words the form of which strongly recalls their Latin origin. Etymology is of course considered in the " learned " formation of new words from foreign *roots*, and no scientist or thinker deliberately forming a new technical term would attach a Latin prefix to a Greek root, or a Greek prefix to a Latin root. But for popular purposes, hybrid words easily gain currency, *e.g.*, *bicycle*, *television*,* one reason no doubt being that the prefixes used are well understood and in vogue at a particular time. The use of affixes for combination with existing words is, indeed, a somewhat popular method of word-making. It has been much less employed by scholars and grammarians than by poets, journalists and everyday folk. Certain affixes have

* *Bi-cycle* is Latin and Greek ; *tele-vision* is Greek and French. Many alternatives of pure Greek origin have been suggested for " television," *e.g.*, *telourama*, *teleopsis*, *telephany* ; but it seems probable that the " hybrid " will survive.

enjoyed a temporary vogue and have been used to create compounds of merely local or short-lived currency. It is curious, for example, how many words ending with the suffix -*less* are first recorded in poetry : some at least must have been created by poets. Thus *woundless* is first found in Spenser ; *limitless* in Sidney ; *waveless* in Peele ; *resistless* in Marlowe ; *soundless*, *dauntless* and *spiritless* in Shakespeare ; *realmless* and *lashless* in Keats ; *fleckless* in Tennyson. Similarly, as has been mentioned elsewhere, the prefix *a-* (=on) was freely employed to make new compounds by poets of the Nineteenth Century, as in *achill*, *adangle*, *aflicker*, *aflower*. The Latin prefix *dis-* was particularly active in the Sixteenth and Seventeenth Centuries, when such compounds were created as *discage*, *dischurch*, *discloak*, *disedge*, *dislimn*, *disquantity*, and many more. During the last hundred and fifty years or so, the suffixes -*ism*, -*ist*, -*istic*, all primarily of Greek origin, have been widely employed by publicists and others in discussing movements of thought and their leaders. As examples may be named *collectivism*, *conservatism*, *opportunism*, *realism* ; *alarmist*, *capitalist*, *nihilist* ; *formulistic*, *quietistic*, *realistic*. The suffix -*y* (A.S. *ig*) played an important part in the Fourteenth Century in forming such useful adjectives as *angry*, *hearty*, *milky* ; in its most recent career it has been largely used in various trivial and colloquial formations such as *bumpy*, *messy*, *oniony*. Sometimes a particular affix has a certain stylistic quality. Some of Carlyle's sardonic humour, for instance, is certainly expressed by the prefix in his string of epithets *bediademed*, *becoronetted*, *bemitred*; and in Ruskin's aesthetic criticism formations in *-esque*, such as *Turneresque*, are characteristic. The use of affixes in combination with existing words is, indeed, a matter of literary and common usage; it is not controlled by grammarians. Educated opinion exercises some sort of supervision, and is perhaps becoming more conscious of its duties and powers. Although superfluous compounds sooner or later die a natural death, those persons who care for the purity of the language should avoid loading an overstocked vocabulary with words so easily made and often so useless.

IV

English is fortunate in possessing the means of easily absorbing words of Greek and Latin origin into its vocabulary. The varied and numerous French words received into the language during the three centuries after the Norman Conquest represented many types of derivation from Latin. A glance at a Chaucer Glossary in which the terminations *-able*, *-ent*, *-ible*, *-ion*, *-ive*, *-ous* and various others occur will illustrate this point.

The French words provided a pattern according to which derivatives drawn directly from Latin could be fashioned, and as early as the Fourteenth Century this was beginning to be done. In consequence, English contains many words whose similarity of form disguises a difference of origin. For instance, the verb *reclaim* was borrowed from French, but *declaim* was formed directly from the Latin " declamare."

The terminations adopted in Latin derivatives have been fixed not by system but by usage, and they often appear inconsistent. For example, *existence*, from the third conjugation verb " existere," has the Latin termination *-ence*, while *resistance*, also from a third conjugation verb, " resistere," has the French termination *-ance*. Sometimes a termination has been lost, as in *robust*, which has ousted *robustious*; sometimes one has been added, as in *submissive*, which has replaced *submiss*. Verbs of Latin origin were at first based on the infinitive, as in French; but by degrees it became a common practice to form derivatives from the participial stem, as in *separate, expedite*. *Prepare* and *declare* follow the older method, and many similar forms were once current, *e.g., accumule, annihil, decore, vituper,* which are found in Caxton, as well as *extirp, promulge, confeder,* which are later. This change in the formation of verbs was perhaps connected, either as cause or effect, with a tendency to regard such words as *alienate,* *felicitate*, *infect*, when used as passive participles, as pedantic and un-English. The dividing line comes in the Seventeenth Century ; and in the age of Dryden, the practice with respect to Latin derivatives is noticeably more " modern " than in the age of Milton and Browne.

V

Just as the derivation of words from Latin was rendered easy by the French element in the language, so the Latin element prepared the way for the formation of new derivatives from Greek. The Romans themselves, who borrowed many Greek words, adopted a system of equivalents for certain diphthongs and consonants which their language did not possess. Thus αι was rendered by *ae* ; ει by *i* ; οι by *œ* ; ου by *u* ; υ by *y* ; κ by *c* ; θ by *th* ; φ by *ph* ; χ by *ch* ; ψ by *ps* ; ρ by *rh*. On this system Greek derivatives have been naturalized in English, whether drawn direct from Greek or through the medium of Latin. Thus " kuklos " is represented by *cycle* ; " eidolon " by *idol* ; " kunosoura " by *cynosure*, etc. Derivatives formed without reference to the Latin system of vowels, *e.g.*, *oneirocritical*,* are rare, though certain recent writers, *e.g.*, Browning, have sometimes transliterated proper

* *i.e.*, " practising the interpretation of dreams." The French is " onirocritique."

names in this way (*e.g.*, Hephaistos, Alkestis). The popular tendency, however, has been to anglicize as much as possible, and even the Latin diphthong *œ* is now rarely used; thus the older *œconomy* has been generally replaced by *economy*. This seems to be a movement in the right direction, for, as large numbers of new words are continually being derived from Greek, it is desirable that they should agree in form as much as possible with English usage.

CHAPTER VII
CHANGES IN MEANING

THE principal use of words is to convey a meaning, and the changes to which their meaning is liable form the most philosophical topic in the history of language. Much of what has been said elsewhere in this book might fitly be repeated in the present chapter, for the history of almost every word is in part the history of its meaning. The subject is as delicate as it is wide. It has been said that no word is used twice in precisely the same sense, and in view of the infinitely complex associations in the mind of every speaker, this is scarcely an exaggeration. Some words convey so much, that a whole book might be written on their meaning ; and indeed many thinkers have toiled long on the definition of small words such as, *good, beautiful, sublime, romantic*. It was well said by Cardinal Newman that the word *God* is itself a theology, and there are hundreds of other words which are in themselves embryonic systems of thought. To deal at all with the vast subject of meaning, the philologist must limit his view. Ignoring the history of individual words, he must consider the principal ways in which changes in meaning have affected the vocabulary. Some words, which would otherwise have perished, have been preserved for the sake of a new and definite meaning. Some, in order to meet the constant changes in thought and the progress of knowledge, have had fresh functions assigned to them. New words may be manufactured at any time ; but a change in the meaning of an existing word is often a simpler and more convenient way of supplying a need. The process is one of the most ancient and the most natural in the growth of language.

I

A simple but also a striking illustration of change in meaning is provided by the large group of words developed from proper names. Quite a number of English words, not only nouns but also verbs and adjectives, are derived from the names of countries, towns and persons. Sometimes the name of a man, whether historical or fictitious, noted for some act or quality, has been extended without change of form into a word of general use. Thus, the appellation *Mentor* has been borrowed from the name of the adviser of Telemachus in the *Odyssey*, or perhaps rather from that of a similar character in Fénelon's *Télémaque*, and may now be applied to any counsellor. This is a clear instance of generalization. But very often names are extended in a less direct manner by some form of association. Thus the name of *Derrick*, a Tyburn hangman who flourished about 1600, was extended not to other persons of his profession, but to a contrivance for hoisting heavy weights. Also, by association, a one-horse closed carriage in vogue about 1850 was called a *brougham* from the name of a well-known peer. The verb *to burke* originates in the name of a murderer who suffocated or strangled his victims. The noun *mackintosh* commemorates, in slightly altered form, the name of its inventor, Charles Macintosh. *Sandwich* preserves the memory of an Eighteenth Century earl who once spent twenty-four hours at the gaming-table, sustained only by light refreshment. *Pinchbeck*, originally the name of a watch-maker, was afterwards applied to an alloy of copper and zinc designed to resemble gold, and was later employed as an adjective meaning "sham" or "spurious." The word *greengage* is a composition of " green " and the surname of a certain Sir William Gage, an early cultivator of the fruit. Place-names have entered our vocabulary in large numbers, often in an altered form. *Meander*, both noun and verb, is originally derived from the name of a winding river in Phrygia. *Canary* has given birth at various times to three different names : that of a Spanish dance, of a sweet wine, and of a yellow bird. A good instance of the effect of association is given by the development of the word *Atlas* into a common noun. The change is due to a representation of Atlas supporting the heavens which appeared as a frontispiece in early atlases. *Calico* is derived ultimately from " Calicut " ; *cambric* from "Cambray"; *copper* from " Cyprus"; *cravat* from " Croatia " ; *damask* from " Damascus " ; *florin* from " Florence"; *gipsy* from " Egypt"; *indigo* from "India"; *jet* from " Gagae "; *milliner* from " Milan"; *muslin* from "Mosul"; *nankeen* from " Nankin"; *pistol* from " Pistoia"; *polony* from " Bologna"; *serge* and *silk* from " Seres", the Oriental people, perhaps the Chinese, from whom silk was first obtained by Europeans.

II

The principle underlying the extension of application just illustrated is one of resemblance or association. The first man who, after his Homeric prototype, is called *a* Mentor is conveniently and consciously misnamed. Similarly, such words as *damask* and *silk* were doubtless generalized by being used for some counterfeit article which might easily pass for genuine. Apart from proper names, resemblance is still the principle which leads to word-generalization. An enormous part of our language is founded on metaphor— the transference of a word from its original use to a

I   E.W.

new one based on some likeness or analogy. Many words, first created in a state of a life widely different from ours, have been put to uses which greatly disguise their original function. Probably few persons who use the word *pipe* for one of its many purposes in modern speech, often reflect that the first pipe was a musical instrument in the form of a tube. It was the extension of the word to some other object of similar shape that led to the transformation of its meaning. Since Arcadian days, scores of tubular forms have come into common use, so that the word *pipe* has now to fulfil the most varied functions. We have *organ-pipes, gas-pipes, water-pipes, wind-pipes, tobacco-pipes*; and to this list further compounds could easily be added. Generalization has also greatly increased the functions of our verbs. For instance, *to tease* meant originally " to separate the fibres " of such materials as wool or flax; but for something over three centuries it has been used figuratively in the sense " to worry or irritate "—a meaning tantamount to a new word. Sometimes, the original sense of a word disappears while its secondary sense remains. *To thrill*, for example, originally meant " to penetrate." This meaning is obsolete; but from the figurative sense " to penetrate with some non-material force," *e.g.*, an emotion, was developed the transferred sense " to affect with a sudden wave of emotion "—a use still, of course, quite common. The extent of word-generalization can be best realized by a comparison between the primary functions of certain of our oldest words with those which they perform in modern English. It is perhaps the rule rather than the exception that an ancient noun of Anglo-Saxon origin should have acquired a figurative or transferred meaning besides its literal sense. For an illustration, one has only to run through the names of certain parts of the body. We can speak of the *head* of a College, the *eye* of a needle, the *mouth* of a river, the *tooth* of a saw, the *neck* of a bottle, the *brow* of a hill, the *body* of a church, the *hand* of a clock, the *leg* of a table, the *foot* of a page. Some nouns of this kind have begotten a whole class of new names. A sub-meaning of the word *tongue* is defined by the *Shorter Oxford Dictionary* as " Anything that resembles or suggests the human or animal tongue by its shape, position, function, or use " : some dozen examples are then given, including " a narrow strip of land," " a tapering jet of flame," and " the clapper of a bell." Generalization of this kind is produced by an imaginative treatment of language which is essentially poetic. There is indeed no difference except that made by familiarity between the prose metaphor of " the man *dogs* my footsteps " and the poetic metaphor of Shakespeare's phrase : " the hearts that *spaniel'd* me at heels." Some generalization, however, is due not to figurative ingenuity but to impersonal causes. One of the clearest examples of the widening in sense which certain words undergo with the lapse of time is *coster-monger*. Originally the meaning of this word was " a seller of costard apples." In popular usage this sense has long been forgotten, and the articles which a " coster-monger " is expected to retail in the streets have now, of course, much more variety.

III

Specialization is the converse of generalization : it is the process by which in the course of time certain words, from being applied to a whole class of things come to be applied to a part only of that class. The process is a very natural one in a language which, like English, has been, at many periods in its history, super-fluously rich in synonyms. It provides a use for words which might otherwise have become obsolete. When two words exist for the same thing, it is difficult for both to survive unless their functions are divided : the one remaining the general word, the other having some special duty assigned to it. Anglo-Saxon was abundantly supplied with synonyms for certain words, even before the foreign invasions. To this wealth of language, large portions of three fresh vo-cabularies, the Norse, the French and the Latin, were subsequently added. No doubt this abundance was an advantage in some ways, but for certain purposes of expression it must have been confusing. The poet will welcome a wide choice between words of different sound, length and emotional suggestion ; the thinker will prefer that every word in use shall be capable of strictly intellectual definition. The desire for precision, which grows stronger with the progress of culture and education, drove many words out of use ; it would have discarded still more had they not been saved by specialization.

In Anglo-Saxon the two verbs *gan* and *wadan* meant much the same : the former has survived as *go*, with its original sense almost unchanged, the latter as *wade*, with the specialized meaning, " go through water." Precisely why the sense of *wade* should have been modified in this particular way, no one can explain. Presumably, the change is one of those " contextual developments " not uncommon in the history of language. From its frequent use in connection with water, the habit must have grown, sooner or later, of using the word in no other way. Possibly the need of a special verb was consciously felt, and the change more or less deliberately made. Many other words have undergone a similar change in meaning. For example, *shroud* originally meant " a garment "—a word for which the language provides several synonyms; the modern sense " winding-sheet " dates from the latter half of the Sixteenth Century. Another word for " garment," viz., *weed*, now survives only in connection with the mourning worn by a widow. *Deer* and *fowl* were formerly generic names for " animal " and " bird," the sense still possessed by the cognate " Tier " and " Vogel " of Modern German. The original sense of *starve*, viz., " die," is retained not only in the German " sterben " but in certain English dialects; the phrase " starved with cold,"* for instance, is still sometimes heard. That specialization can take place in quite recent times is shown by the word *sky-scraper*. Within the last century-and-a-half, this epithet could be used of a ship, a horse, and a man; only during the last fifty years has its application been confined to a particularly high building. One of the most striking instances of the process is the change in the meaning of *fulsome*. This adjective, a combination of *full* and *-some* had formerly the most general sense of " excessive." Its present meaning, " offensive to good taste from excess or want of measure " is the only one, out of the seven recorded by the *Oxford English Dictionary*, which has survived.

Though the results of specialization are diverse, the process corresponds to some extent with what is sometimes called the " downward tendency " of language.

* Used hyperbolically, like the phrase, " *dead* with cold."

Certain words lose caste, and from being part of the ordinary language come to be regarded as vulgar, or as contemptuous and abusive. The love of refinement is always selective : there are fashions in words as in all things, and no doubt some words have fallen in repute simply by being forgotten by educated people, so that they become in time the peculiar property of un-learned persons. This may account for the offensive meaning long ascribed to the verb *to stink*, though originally the word had a perfectly neutral sense. The synonym "to smell," which was perhaps more in vogue, may have driven the rival verb into disuse and so into disrepute. To avoid the outspoken term seems to some people a social duty; none the less they continue to express themselves, and thus words once innocent lose their purity. *Lust* was originally a synonym for "pleasure" or "delight," and its mean-ing "illicit pleasure" possibly arose from the com-mon avoidance of a blunter expression. Originally *wench* was an equivalent of "girl" or "maid": this word, too, has lost its status and become degraded. Of the various synonyms for "man" which formerly existed, some have disappeared altogether, and per-haps the only one which survives is *wight*, which could be of no use in the vocabulary but for the half com-passionate, half contemptuous sense which has be-come attached to it. How strongly fashion may operate on language is shown by the strange disesteem into which the verb *occupy* fell at a certain stage of its history. Readers of *Henry IV* will remember Doll Tearsheet's allusion to this fact : " These villains will make the word (captain) as odious as the word *occupy*; which was an excellent good word before it was ill sorted."

IV

It is comparatively seldom that the change in meaning which words have undergone can be adequately summed up by the simple terms, Generalization or Specialization. Many words are subject to both processes at different stages of their history. The adjective *nice*, for example, which is derived through French from the Latin " nescius " (" ignorant ") developed several new meanings during the Sixteenth and Seventeenth Centuries. It could mean " foolish," " wanton," " rare," " coy," " over-refined." Only the last of these meanings survived into the Eighteenth Century, and for about fifty years, the prevailing sense was " difficult to please or satisfy." Anyone using the words " he is not nice " about 1750 would certainly have meant, " he is not fastidious." But during the reign of George III, manners were becoming more refined and " particular," hence the word *nice* becomes a term of praise. In the year 1769 occurs the first recorded use of the adjective in the sense " agreeable," " delightful." Since that time the word has been generalized into an almost meaningless term of praise or approval,* and its older sense survives only in rare use and in a few such phrases as " a nice distinction."

Another instance of alternate widening and narrowing of meaning is provided by the noun *panel*. To understand the history of this word, one must remember that its origin is the mediaeval Latin *pannellus*, a diminutive of *pannus*. *Pannus* originally meant " a piece of cloth "; but introduced through French into English as *pane*, it was widely generalized, and at one time could signify " a piece, portion or side of anything." Of this wide use, only a few senses now survive, of which the most familiar is " a division of a window." The history of *panel* has been parallel to that of *pane*, but somewhat more complicated. It first developed three principal meanings : (1) " a piece of cloth," (2) " a small piece or slip of parchment," (3) " a distinct portion of some surface." From the second of these senses a special meaning soon emerged, viz., " the slip of parchment on which the sheriff entered the names of jurors." Next the word *panel* was used for the list of jurymen itself. Its mean-

* Cf. *Northanger Abbey*, Ch. xiv. " Very true," said Henry, " and this is a very nice day ; and we are taking a very nice walk ; and you are two very nice young ladies. Oh, it is a very nice word, indeed !—it does for everything."

ing was then extended by transference to " any list of men, or of beasts." In 1913 a new sense was formed by specialization : " a list of doctors who are prepared to accept as patients persons registered under the National Health Insurance Acts," and in contemporary English this is one of the prevailing uses. From the third of the original senses various meanings have survived, of which the most familiar is " a distinct compartment of a door, shutter or the like." The history of the word has thus been a series of expansions and contractions.

V

One test of the quality of a language is its success in expressing distinctions of meaning. Many words can take on a special sense from their context, but it is an obvious advantage that differences of meaning should be indicated by differences of form. To the past writers of English, known and unknown, we owe a number of useful *differentiations*, by which various uses of the same word are distinguished by differences of form or spelling. A simple illustration of the process is provided by the pair of words *to* and *too*. Those words were originally the same ; and the spelling of the latter indicates merely a stressed form of *to*. *To* has remained the spelling of the preposition, *too* has become the form of the adverb developed from it.

Similarly, *off* was originally a variant spelling of the preposition *of*, the functions of the former word being an offshoot from those of the latter. *Through* and *thorough* were also, in the first place, variant spellings; indeed, *thorough* survives in some fairly recent verse as an alternative form. The common sense of *thorough*, however, developed from such expressions as "thorough-going," *i.e.*, going *through*, affecting every part or detail of something.

The irregularity of English spelling in the past has no doubt been a frequent stumbling-block; but it was many times turned to good account and has enriched our vocabulary with scores of words which are now quite indispensable. *Human* and *humane* were formerly two spellings of the same word; but, from about 1790, the need for an adjective corresponding to certain senses of the Latin " humanus " led to the appropriation of *humane* to this use. The history of *urban* and *urbane* is similar; the latter form had originally to do duty for both forms as now used, and *urban* was rare before the Nineteenth Century. Again, the distinction between *flour* and *flower* was formerly one of mere spelling, until the specific use of *flour* for the " flower " or finest part of the meal created what was in effect a new word. *Curtsey* was originally a variant of *courtesy* : from the Sixteenth Century it has been applied to the " courtesy " of a woman's obeisance.

Council and *counsel*, though of different origin, were confused during the era of greatest uncertainty in spelling, and it was not until the Sixteenth Century that the present distinction was clearly established. *Die* and *dye*, though also of different sources, were long confused, and the present distinction is more recent even than the time of Dr. Johnson, who spells both verbs " die." *Posy* was originally a syncopated form of " poesy," and was applied to such tokens as the motto or " posy " of a ring, until by an extension of meaning it signified a nosegay or bouquet. *Mettle* (meaning " quality of disposition or temperament ") is a differentiation of *metal*; *mantel* of *mantle*; *travel* of *travail*. It is only by a fortunate accident that we possess both of the nouns *tone* and *tune*, for the latter is apparently no more than an unexplained altera-tion of " tone " current in late Middle English. The differentiation between *born* and *borne* corresponds to the two possible senses of " bear "; *born* meaning " brought forth as offspring," *borne* meaning " carried." Other differentiations, based on alternative spellings, are *draft* and *draught*, *sergeant* and *serjeant*, *spirt* and *spurt*.

Differentiation has sometimes been founded on other distinctions than that of alternative spelling. For example, the words *temporal* and *temporary*, though descended from different Latin adjectives, were, for a part of their history, used as synonyms. But the best usage certainly requires that *temporal* should imply a contrast with " eternal " or " spiritual," and that *temporary* should mean " lasting for a limited time." Again, difference of accentuation has sometimes led to distinction of meaning. In the course of time the accent of many English words has shifted backwards, in agreement with the tendency to stress the initial syllable. Thus, *dragon* and *dragoon* (the second word being originally applied to a kind of carbine because it " breathes fire ") are descended from the same source, but correspond respectively to the newer and older forms of the word ; *salon* (which has kept its French pronunciation) and *saloon* are a similar pair. *Genteel* is a re-adoption of the French " gentil," which had entered the language earlier, and had assumed the form *gentle*. Various distinctions of meaning have also been founded on the different form of an affix. For instance, *uninterested* bore, for the first century of its career as an English word, the sense now confined to *disinterested*. Nor was the distinction between *excellence* and *excellency* properly established until the end of the Eighteenth Century. Still more recent is the differentiation of *sailor* and *sailer* ; previously the two forms could be used indiscriminately, though *sailor* now properly signifies " a professional seaman," while *sailer* means simply " one who sails." The useful adjective *sensuous* was apparently coined by Milton, who wished for a word free from the implications of *sensual*, and the distinction has gained currency through its adoption by other writers, such as Coleridge. Milton, who was closely attentive to differences of form and meaning in words, may also have founded the distinction between *visitor* and *visitant*; in any case, *Paradise Lost* contains the first known instance of *visitant* in its current sense of " a supernatural visitor." The distinction between these two nouns is finely illustrated in R. L. Stevenson's story *Markheim*, where the apparition who surprises the murderer after his deed, is called successively a " visitor " and a " visitant," as if to suggest an existence on the borderline of the natural and the supernatural.

CHAPTER VIII

THE HISTORICAL DEVELOPMENT OF THE VOCABULARY, 1500-1800

THE three centuries which lie between 1500 and 1800 constitute a fairly well-marked division in the history of our language. At the beginning of the period are two events of signal importance to the life of the nation : the severance of the Church of England from the Roman obedience, and the rise of a single dialect to pre-eminence among the rest. These events which both took place gradually are roughly contemporary, and are among the principal signs that the Middle Ages were at an end and that a new phase of our history had begun. The end of the epoch is scarcely less clearly marked. By 1800, the Industrial Revolution which converted England from a rural nation into one of town-dwellers was in full progress, and the rise of democracy in Europe which was destined to transform slowly but surely nearly all our ancient institutions had been signalised by the great events of 1789. Before 1500, England was a part of Catholic Europe; since 1800, she has played an ever-increasing part in world-politics. Between these two dates she developed her national character in unregretful isolation from the rest of mankind. Religion first and then party-politics were her absorbing passions; and towards the end of the epoch, " in a fit of absent-mindedness," she founded a world-wide empire. The struggle of conscience with conscience, and of party with party, has left its trace no less in the works of Spenser and Milton, of Dryden and Swift, than in the trash of the forgotten scribbler. The choice between Protestant and Catholic, Parliament and King, Whig and Tory, was forced on succeeding generations : naturally, the rival passions left their mark on the literature and language of the nation. Words, like swords, are weapons of war : they are also symbols of love and reverence; of hatred and contempt ; of the virtues and vices of human society. Between 1500 and 1800, many new words were added to the vocabulary by composition, by derivation, and by adoption from foreign languages. But by far the most interesting are those which are coloured by fresh associations from the vigorous life of the nation. These, whether new or old, form the chief contribution to our vocabulary during the three centuries.

I

Among the first-fruits of the Reformation were Tindale's translations from the Bible; and with Tindale began that long effort of the Protestant and Puritan to speak a peculiar language, purged from ungodliness and superstition. Tindale, whose translation of the New Testament appeared in 1526, was a scholar and an extreme Protestant : both qualities are shown in his choice of words. To Tindale we owe the word *elder* as a literal and non-Catholic equivalent of the Greek word previously rendered as " priest "; to Tindale also is due the Puritan use of *congregation* in preference to " church." * The modern sense of *godly* is first found in Tindale ; so too are the new derivatives *ungodly*, *godless* and *godliness*. Such " precision " was quickly noted by the opposite party, and a double-edged vocabulary of criticism and contempt began to be formed. *Scruple*, *scrupulosity*, and *scrupulousness* are among the earliest words of this class : all are first recorded in 1526. In More's *Confutation of Tindale* (1532) appears the first known use of *factious*, in the phrase, " his false factious heresies "; but on the whole the Reforming Party seems to have had the more prolific gift for verbal abuse. *Weakling* was apparently suggested to Tindale by Luther's " weichling ": and words of a similar type, *e.g.*, *popeling* (a papist), *worldling* and *shaveling*, were soon added to the Protestant vocabulary. The last of these words, " a

* Cf. " Apon this roocke I wyll bylde my congregcion." Tindale's translation of Matt. xvi. 18.

contemptuous epithet for a tonsured ecclesiastic," was one of a large class, of which *abbey-lubber* (1538) and *mass-monger* (1550) are specimens. *Sincere* was a word which the Protestants appropriated to themselves, being in its first known use applied to Wyclif (1533); *lazy* * (1549) and *foolery* † (1522) were used to belabour their enemies. *Changeling* and *turn-coat* significantly appear in 1555 and 1557, when the conscience of many Protestants was being put to the test under Mary Tudor ; and *time-server* (1584) is another compound belonging to that century of unfixed principles. The religious controversies of the age are commemorated in a plentiful crop of words which once stirred fervid passions ; *papish*, *papist*, *papistic*, *papistical*, and *papistry* (all hostile or opprobrious words) appear in the first half of the Sixteenth Century, and to the same period belongs the stern Calvinistic *reprobate*, in its original sense of " one rejected by God." Various words, too, which now have a more general application were once weapons of religious warfare : thus *epicure* was used about 1550 almost in the sense of "atheist"; *libertine* meant "an antinomian in religion " ; and in the next century, *rationalist* first

---

* " Those laysy lubbers and popyshe bellygoddes." (Bale.)

† " It is not that [ringing of bells] that will serue against yᵉ deuill : yet we haue belieued such fooleries in tymes past." (Latimer.)

appeared as a label to distinguish a certain sect from the Presbyterians and Independents. It is a relief to find, amid this ferment of rival creeds, the tolerant Hooker administering a gentle rebuke in his epithet *over-scrupulous* (1597).

Simplicity in demeanour, a biblical sobriety in language were the outward marks of the early Puritans; and various traces of their unworldliness remain in our vocabulary. Their favourite use of the word *fine* in the sense of "dainty" or "fastidious" is now rare or obsolete; but its derivative *finical* (1592) is still in use, so too is the verb *flaunt* (1566), used by such critics of manners as Gascoigne in his *Steele Glasse* and Stubbes in his *Anatomie of Abuses*. The desire to avoid "superstition" revealed itself, during the Sixteenth Century, in the clear differentiation between *holiday* and *holyday*, and later in the preference of terms such as *Christtide* and *Lord's Day* to "Christmas" and "Sunday." *Sabbatarian* came into use about 1620 ("none of your precise sabbatarians"), and various derivatives from "scripture," such as *scriptural*, *scripturist*, and *scriptuarian*, appear later in the century. The nobler side of Puritanism, its deep sense of moral responsibility, and its habit of rigorous self-examination appear in various derivatives from "conscience," *e.g.*, *conscientious* (1611) and *conscientiousness* (1631). But the fullest revelation of this side of the Puritan character occurs in a large group of words beginning with *self-*. The adjective *selfish* is recorded in 1640 : it became popular among the " godly," and was denounced by their enemies as being of the Presbyterians' " own new mint." Other formations followed in quick succession : *self-denial* * and *selfishness* within the next four years ; *self-interest*, *self-confidence*, *self-applauding*, *self-esteem*, with many others, a little later. Fresh compounds were formed after 1660, but, as one would expect from the changed character of the age, many of these indicate a critical rather than an introspective attitude. Examples are *self-centred* (1676), *self-righteous* (1680), and *self-satisfied* (1734). During the Civil Wars and the rule of Cromwell, the ways of the victorious " saints " were attacked by various abusive words, some of which are still current. Their love of pulpit oratory gave rise to *tub-preacher* ; their democratic theories to *leveller*, and their alleged hypocrisy to the contemptuous *canter*. Many of the nicknames bestowed on the Puritans have been long since forgotten, or survive only in the mocking lines of Butler's *Hudibras*.

II

That the effect of the Renaissance on our vocabulary was on the whole salutary is due to a number of causes,

* " The Self-Denying Ordinance " of the Parliamentarian Army was passed in 1644.

of which one of the chief was the vitality of our popular literature. It is true that many scholars of the time, fresh from contemplating the literary splendour of the " classics," felt a certain pity or contempt for the vernacular. Fortunately, however, there were urgent practical reasons why the study of good English could not be wholly neglected. The creation of a new liturgy, which should be accurate, comprehensive and intelligible, was a task which compelled some of the best minds of the Sixteenth Century to weigh the use and meaning of English words with the utmost nicety. At the same time, the translation of the Bible fixed the attention of scholars scarcely less on the work of their English predecessors than on the language of the original texts. The Authorized Version is the work not of an age, but of many centuries ; and its authority as an English classic is due largely to its preservation of the traditions of our language. The popular drama was another bulwark against pedantry. It is true that in many of the best plays the language is not always simple. Shakespeare is often highly compressed and " poetic " in style ; Jonson, as Dryden remarks, " Latinizes too much." None the less, the taste of a popular audience had to be considered ; many dramatists wrote primarily for " the City," and though the plays of the period contain every variety of style, the idiomatic English of everyday use, handled often with literary deftness, is the most constant element, and is hostile to affectation, whether courtly or pedantic. In spite of all, however, too many words of foreign derivation were introduced during the Sixteenth Century and the first half of the Seventeenth. Mingled with many well-formed words of classical origin which are a true enrichment of the language are others which are both needless and uncouth. It was the great antiquary of the age, John Selden, who remarked : " We have more words than notions, half a dozen words for the same thing."

Words of Latin origin had been entering our language for centuries ; but many of these had been useful or necessary additions. As early as the Fifteenth Century there were signs of affectation, *e.g.*, the use of " visually perceive " for " see." * This was the beginning of a movement which lasted till about 1660, when the vogue of erudition gave place to the vogue of politeness. But the earlier prose-writers of the Tudor period generally employed a sober vocabulary without ostentatious learning. They had, however, the practice of introducing, when necessary, Greek and Latin words of technical meaning without change : many of these survive. Thus, Elyot uses *acumen* in 1531 ; More *apostrophe* in 1533 ; Ascham, *decorum* and *acme* about 1568. The writers who naturalized the

* Chambers, *Continuity of English Prose*, p. cxvi.

much-needed terms of literary criticism in the last years of the century sometimes followed this example ; others anglicized their words. Many words like *epic*, *climax*, and *onomatopoeia* came first into use from the works of Puttenham and his contemporaries. *Emphasis* and *energy*, both, in the first place, words of literary criticism, also belong to the late Sixteenth Century. A little later, Bacon resumed the task, which had already made progress in the age of Chaucer, of founding the vocabulary of philosophy and natural science. For his technical terms he generally uses words derived from Latin or Greek. Thus the adjective *acid* from " acidus " (" sour ") occurs in his *Sylva*; *acoustic*, from Greek by way of French, occurs in *The Advancement of Learning*. To describe the general tendency of his philosophy which aimed at " the relief of man's estate " he invents the word *melioration* : " You must ever resort to the beginning of things for melioration." Other scientific words to which he gave currency are *epidermis*, *lapidification*, *ligneous*. An interesting reminder of his method of enquiry is the adjective *crucial*, from his phrase " instantia crucis," on which later thinkers modelled such expressions as " crucial instance " and " crucial experiment." Another characteristic invention is the now prevalent sense of *collate* : " to bring together for comparison." These few examples give some slight

hint of Bacon's contribution to thought. A study of
his diction would also indicate his greatness as a
stylist; for in an age when learned men too often
made a vain display of erudition, Bacon's use of words
is in the last degree economical. He has little or no
preference for Latinisms as such; rather, he is in-
genious in extending the use of native words; for
instance, the apt and simple term *creeper*, for a trailing
or climbing plant, is first recorded in his *Sylva* (1626).
In a mixed language like English, however, it is natural
that technical words should be drawn mostly from
foreign sources. There were, too, many gaps in our
ordinary language which were best filled by derivatives from Greek or Latin; and an important task in
word-making remained to be performed by those
erudite prose-writers of the age whose style echoes in
every sentence some line or phrase from a classical
author. Of these masters of scholarly prose, Sir
Thomas Browne is a typical representative. The pages
of his books, especially of the *Pseudodoxia Epidemica*
(1646), abound in words newly formed from Greek
and Latin, of which the following specimens both suggest the quality of his style and indicate his importance
in the history of our language : *antediluvian, approxi-
mate, ascetic, carnivorous, causation, deleterious, facti-
tious, precarious, retrogression*. In prose contemporary
with Browne's are first found *appreciation, concatena-*

tion, concomitant, circumnavigate, criterion, fluctuation, dispel, hallucinate, lambent, longevity, loquacity, hesitate, heterodox, scintillate, torpid, ultimate, valediction, and many others of greater length, to which Restoration writers fitly applied the Horatian epithet " sesquipedalian." *

One of the consequences of the Renaissance was a haunting fear that the vernaculars were not destined to survive. Bacon had this feeling. " These modern languages," he wrote, " will at one time or other, play the bankrupts with books." Bacon, however, knew that English had its appropriate idiom, and that nothing was so likely to perish as a compromise between two languages which missed the spirit of both. Not all men of the age were as wise ; many, indeed, whose inclination leant towards the conscious cultivation of " style," held that the one thing to be avoided was simple English. Thomas Wilson, author of the *Art of Rhetoric* (1553), protests against " ink-horn " terms and the " foolish fantastical who Latin their tongues," and he quotes as a specimen of affectation a letter addressed to a certain gentleman from an aspirant to a vacant benefice. This absurd composition is dated " the penult of the month sextile," † and contains

* " Sesquipedalia verba," *i.e.* words a foot and a half long, *Ars Poetica,* 97.

† i.e. August 30th.

such sentences as " I obtestate your sublimity to extol mine infirmity. There is a sacerdotal dignity in my native country contignate to me, where I now contemplate, which your workshipful benignity could soon impetrate for me." Unfortunately, the critics of the age were not strong enough to uphold the cause of pure English, and many of the greatest writers who flourished between 1600 and 1660 continued to adopt new words derived from the classical tongues, without distinguishing between the useful and the superfluous. The technical phrase *vernal equinox* which was current in the Sixteenth Century conforms to the established type in English usage ; but the habit which grew up about 1610 of substituting *vernal* for the adjective " spring " or " spring-like " in ordinary descriptive contexts is often enough pure pedantry. Similarly, *hibernal,* as a rhetorical synonym for " wintry " or " late," appears in the prose both of Bishop Andrewes in 1626 and of Sir Thomas Browne twenty years later : whether the word is ever quite admissible in English is perhaps an open question. No doubt such words may add a touch of verbal beauty or distinction to a single poetic context, as in Milton's line,

Or sight of vernal bloom, or summer's rose,*

but their merit lies in their rarity : they do not wear well, and to use them is to place the means of corrupt-

* *Paradise Lost*, iii. 43.

ing the language within the reach of the unskilful.
Examples of such language could be multiplied end-
lessly. Every reader of Jacobean and Caroline prose is
aware how often an otherwise fine effect is marred by
an excessive admixture of " ink-horn " terms. At a
time when Shakespeare was writing prose which
scarcely " dates " after the lapse of three centuries,
Burton in his *Anatomy of Melancholy* (1621) was showing in sentence after sentence his disrespect for native
usage. A very few pages prove how much this writer
would have benefited from realizing that his own
language was already a language with a history. Thus,
he introduces, unchanged, the Latin word *praecipitium*
instead of naturalizing it in the French form, *precipice.*
Deject he uses in its Latin sense of " throw down," not
in its already acquired sense of " dishearten." Past
participles of the form *continuate* are preferred to those
of the form " continued." Newly or recently coined
Latinisms, like *hirsute* (shaggy) and *venditate* (to set out
as if for sale) abound. Such language was the fashion
of the learned, and the work of Sir Thomas Browne
illustrates, scarcely less than Burton's, how the Renaissance threatened the continuity of our prose-traditions.
Mingled with many new words of Latin origin which
have enriched the language are others, still more
numerous, which have deservedly sunk into oblivion.
A candid reader of Browne must admit that the use of

words so uncouth as *aberrancy, aggelation, alary, alliciency, decumbence, salinous, sapidity*, is a constant and characteristic feature of his style. In the prose of Milton, words of learned origin are sometimes used to express polemical contempt : " What can be gathered hence but that the Prelate would still sacrifice ? conceive him, readers, he would *missificate*." * This use of Latinisms in Puritan controversy helped to provoke the reaction ; and it is perhaps characteristic of our history that a literary reform which the good sense of the nation could not achieve was accomplished by a political revolution. On his return from France in 1660, Charles II introduced a love of sprightliness and ease, hostile to formality. Learned words were now associated with the fallen tyrants of the " Old Cause," and a chapter in the history of English style is closed when Butler puts into the mouth of Hudibras such monstrosities as *averruncate, equenecessary, vitilitigation* and *cynarctomachy*.†

Attempts to refashion our spelling, so as to bring certain words into visible relation with the classical tongues, were made under the influence of the Renaissance. In the word *fault* the *-l-* is an intrusive letter from " fallo," introduced into the French form

* *Reason of Church Government*, v. *Missificate* means " celebrate the Mass."

† *i.e.* " a fight between a dog and a bear."

" faute," by writers of the Fifteenth Century. As late as the Eighteenth Century, the -*l*- was mute in ordinary pronunciation, a fact easily illustrated from the rhymes of contemporary poets, as in Goldsmith's couplet :

> Yet he was kind, or if severe in aught,
> The love he bore to learning was in fault.

The impossible form *chirurgeon*, in which the Anglo-French " surgien " is tortured into acknowledging its relation with the Greek " cheirourgia," bears the hall-mark of Sixteenth Century pedantry ; similarly, *rime* was re-fashioned into *rhyme*, to reveal its connection with " rhythmus." The forms *scissors* and *scythe* are a perversion of the Middle English " sisours " and " sithe," due to the erroneous notion that they are connected with the Latin " scindo," and the spelling *island* is an equally mistaken alteration of the native " iland," due to its imaginary relation with " isle " and " insula."

III

The Renaissance left our language better equipped for the expression of abstract ideas and for the purposes of history, criticism, controversy and general culture. This result we owe to the learned men who, while using their native language, expanded its range by drawing on the vocabulary of the classical tongues with a freedom which, though often injudicious, was at least unconscious of its own excess. With all the good they did, however, they must be held accountable for weakening the tradition of pure English and for establishing a foreign tradition, which though often in abeyance has revived with mischievous effect more than once since their time. The disproportionate attention long given in English education to classical studies is partly responsible for this result. When Dr. Johnson applied himself to lexicography, he was exposed to dangers very like those which misled men like Burton and Browne. He fell a victim to his own "scholarship," and loaded his style with learned words. Only in the excitement of conversation did he reveal at times his mastery of plain English, and his training in the admirable school of Addison and Swift. How baneful his influence upon persons of slender education could be, the well-known case of Fanny Burney sufficiently proves. Macaulay's examples of the " Johnsonese " into which Miss Burney fell in her later work, after abandoning the simplicity of *Evelina*, though well known, are perennially amusing: "An offence punishable with imprisonment is, in this language, an offence ' which produces incarceration.' To be starved to death is ' to sink from inanition into nonentity.' Sir Isaac Newton is ' the developer of the skies in their embodied movement '; and Mrs. Thrale, when a party of clever people sat silent, is said to have been ' provoked by the dulness of a taciturnity that in the midst of such renowned interlocutors, produced as narcotic a torpor as could have been caused by a dearth the most barren of all human faculties.'" When, in the next generation, a certain Alderman wished to change the simplicity of Canning's epitaph on Pitt, "He died poor," into "He expired in indigent circumstances," he was showing the same distrust of natural idiom, a distrust which to this day so often betrays the half-educated. Even Scott lapses into journalese when he is careless, as in his use of the adjective *matutinal* for "morning." Matters, however, have on the whole improved since 1660. It is the great praise of Dryden, Cowley and their contemporaries that they established or renewed a tradition of natural English strong enough to vindicate itself when attacked. Even in his own day Dr. Johnson's polysyllables were parodied in such writings as the Dialogue *Lexiphanes*, and the offences of modern journalism do not impose on the educated reader.

To make our language a fitter instrument for the purposes of social intercourse, to adapt it to the needs of easy and elegant prose, to bring it into touch with the everyday life of the nation, was the endeavour of the century which followed the Restoration. The influence of the polite world, and especially of the Court, had acted intermittently on our vocabulary in the past, but it was never so strong as in the reign of Charles II. Under Elizabeth and the first two Stuarts, all spheres of life had their own vitality ; and neither the merchants of the City nor the gentry of the manor-house cared to ape the affectations of the Court. The plays of the period are full of allusions to the social signific- ance of language, and among the plain folk of the City there was enough self-respect to make them keep their own homely diction. Thus, in Middleton's *Chaste Maid in Cheapside* (1630), a goldsmith protests against the fashionable terms addressed to his daughter :

> Pish, stop your words, good knight,—'twill make her
>   blush else— . . .
> Honour and faithful servant ! they are compliments
> For the worthies of Whitehall and Greenwich :
> E'en plain, sufficient, subsidy words serves (*sic*) us, sir.

Puritanism put a stop to the City plays, and reduced the culture of its adherents to something like bareness. The drama had been an admirable school for the cultivation of natural English, and the closing of the theatres was a calamity for the language. At the Restoration there was a desire to blot out all that savoured of the immediate past ; and, as the Common- wealth was associated with cant and pedantry, sim- plicity of style was again in request. This tendency was strengthened by the Royal Society, which encouraged its members to use a "close, naked, natural way of speaking; positive expressions, clear senses, a native easiness, bringing all things as near the mathematical plainness as they can; and preferring the language of artisans, countrymen and merchants before that of wits and scholars." But the spirit of the Restoration could not submit to this sober prescription. The courtiers paid lip-service to "ease" and "nature," but they loved wit and impudence more than plain truth, and they were soon indulging in verbal novelties far removed from the plan proposed by the Royal Society. Many of the favourite words of the age were pure slang, and were acceptable on that very account. Short informal words are the characteristic contribution of the time to our language. *Banter* and *crony* are first recorded in the reign of Charles II. *Sham* appears about 1677, and was much used during the excitement of the Popish Plot. The abusive term *whig* was applied to the promoters of the Exclusion Bill in 1679 and was soon the accepted badge of a great political party. *Prig* came into use as "a vague term of disrespect" about the same time. *Chum* is first recorded in 1684, *fun* in 1685, *mob* in 1688. Swift protested against the spread of new popular words,* especially against the

* " I have done my utmost to stop the Progress of Mobb and Banter " (Swift).

"barbarity which delights in monosyllables." But there seems to have been small opposition to the movement until the great campaign against "low" language in which both Johnson and Chesterfield played an energetic part.

Equally typical of the Restoration was its love of French words and idioms. The gallicizing movement began somewhat before 1660, but it did not gather force until the reign of Charles II. The word *raillery* is noted in 1653 as being "now grown here so common with the better sort." *Coquetterie* and *chagrin* are found in 1656; *risk, caprice, en passant, double entendre, dishabille, faux pas, couchée, éclat, à propos,* occur somewhat later in the century. The rage for new French expressions is satirized in Dryden's *Marriage a la Mode* (1673), in which a certain lady of the Court named Melantha seeks to earn a reputation by the number and novelty of her gallicisms. *Devoirs, good graces, repartee* help to give her language a fashionable flavour. *Embarrass* she describes as "delicious," and her sentence, "I fear they have found my *foible* and will turn me into *ridicule*" introduces in one breath two French words into our language. It is notable that many of the words of this period have not been fully merged in the common mass of our vocabulary, and retain a foreign pronunciation. The same is true of many words and idioms introduced in the Eighteenth Century. *Carte blanche* is recorded in 1707; *distrait* in 1711; *connoisseur* in 1714; *critique* in 1720; " on the *qui vive* " in 1726. Lord Chesterfield, who wrote French as readily as English, introduces *début*, *sang-froid*, and *persiflage* between 1750 and 1760. *Fête* and *vignette* stand to the credit of Horace Walpole, so do *douceur* (" bribe "), and the superfluous *chef d'œuvre*. *Passé*, a typical word of polite disparagement, belongs to 1775. On the outbreak of the Revolution, the character of our French borrowings abruptly changed, but early in the Nineteenth Century we began again to adopt from France new words for our vocabulary of criticism and fashion. *Distingué*, for example, is used by Byron, and so too is *longueur*, of which he remarks : " We've not so good a word, but have the thing."

IV

Many of the words borrowed from France indicate a desire to civilize our language according to the best example. The spirit of self-criticism which gave admission to those words was part of a much larger movement which had been growing for generations. The Reformation itself implied the practice of self-examination, in consequence of which many accepted ideas were liable to revision and re-valuation. This critical habit spread gradually into every department of life, and led naturally to the adoption of many new words, and a change in the meaning and association of many old ones. The simplest form of criticism is iconoclasm, and criticism in the history of language often consists merely in degrading a word previously held in high esteem. Even so to-day, *Victorian* is in many contexts not so much the name of an epoch as an epithet of abuse. The Reformers of the Sixteenth Century had scant respect for the teachers of the " Scholastic " Philosophy, and they showed their feelings by the manner in which they treated the name of one of its leading exponents, Duns Scotus (*d.* 1308). Thanks to Tindale and the early Humanists, this once-honoured name now survives as *dunce*. The contempt entertained for the hair-splitting dialectics of the Middle Ages is registered in the new associations of the word *quiddity*. Literally this word means " the essence of a thing," but from the scorn cast by Reformers about 1540 on " sophemes and quyddities," it is now a synonym for " a captious subtlety."

The struggle between King and Parliament was fought out by blows as well as by words, and the subtler arts of verbal warfare were little studied by either side. But after the peace, words had a fuller part to play, and the final triumph of the Cavaliers gave them leisure to practise the full power of verbal insult. *Fanatic* entered our language about 1660 as a term of partisan abuse. Fuller, in that year, observes that " a new word coined, within few months, called fanatics, seemeth well-proportioned to signify the sectaries of our age." Equally significant are some of the contemporary changes in meaning. The strength of the Puritans lay in their conviction of possessing immediate contact with Heaven. Consequently, *enthusiasm* had for them its literal meaning of " inspiration," and an early use of the word in this sense occurs in 1579. But with the victory of their opponents a very different view prevailed, and *enthusiasm* became a convenient word for implying that the Puritans suffered from self-delusion : an instance of the word so used occurs in 1660. Somewhat later a discourse was written to prove " that the Apostles were no *enthusiasts*." Finally, *enthusiasm* was rescued from the contempt into which it had fallen, but at the same time was secularized. The present meaning " rapturous intensity of feeling " is found in 1716. A similar change takes place in the use of *visionary*. Towards the end of the Commonwealth, the word could still mean " obtaining visions," but to Swift, writing in 1727, it means " given to fanciful views." The revolution in thought is suggested with special vividness by the change in the implications of the phrase *man of the world*. To Coverdale, writing in 1535, the expression means " a worldly person " ; to Fielding, writing in 1749, it is a phrase of social commendation, and means " one experienced in the ways of the world."

A far-reaching change is evident in the use and application of language throughout the period which may be somewhat loosely called " the Eighteenth Century." It was an age which cultivated common sense, the spirit of criticism and the social graces with a zest previously unknown in this country. A few key-words may be quoted which express the spirit of the age. In 1711 occurs the first known use of *self-control* in Shaftesbury's *Characteristics*, and the same writer introduces *well-regulated* two years earlier. *Good sense* is first found in the works of Halifax, the " Trimmer," * in 1688, and *sense* as an equivalent for " common sense " occurs in 1684. A distrust of emotion and imagination is traceable in many new words and applications. *Romantic* begins to mean " having no foundation " about 1667, and *common sense* itself is defined perhaps for the first time by a writer named Amherst in 1726. The obsolete phrase *frames and feelings*, used according to the *Oxford English Dictionary* " as a disparaging term for emotional states as a criterion of the reality of spiritual

---

* " A Trimmer, one neither Whigg nor Tory, is a Hater of Anti-Christ, an Abominator of Enthusiasm " (*Character of a Trimmer*, 1682.)

life," was much used during the Eighteenth Century. *Quackery* and *quackism*, both current by 1720, and *clap-trap* (1727), express a blunter form of disparagement. The sceptical terms *free-thought* and *free-thinking* occur in 1692 and 1711. By the side of these words, which illustrate the regard for a cool and well-balanced mind, are many others which indicate the growing esteem for the social graces and the growing habits of social intercourse. *Charming* and *engaging* in their modern senses, and *gallant*, with the meaning " markedly polite to women," belong to the reign of Charles II. Early in the Eighteenth Century, are found *clique* and *coterie*, also *party* in the sense of " gathering." The sum-total of the social virtues is expressed in the new sense given to *considerate*, " duly attentive to the feelings of others," as compared with its meaning " considered," " deliberate." Another striking development appears in the contrast between the " *comfortable* words " of the Liturgy and the *comfortable* of Horace Walpole's Letters.* The fashions of the Restoration did not satisfy the following age, which found many of its manners coarse and loud. The Eighteenth Century was more refined, and its esteem for elegance of speech and manner has given various words and meanings to the language. *Overdressed*, *showy*, and *flash* in the sense of " gaudy or

* " I am as comfortable as possible " (1770).

smart " all indicate this attitude. Decency and refinement were more studied. What now seems the somewhat brutal use of *carcase* for the human body ceased about 1750, and in 1759 occurs the first known instance of *dentist* in place of the older " tooth-drawer." *Vulgarity* and *vulgarism*, previously applied to *ordinary* things, assume their severer meaning between 1740 and 1780. Lord Chesterfield warns his son that " vulgarism in language is a certain characteristic of bad company and a bad education." But perhaps the favourite word of all for the polite disapproval of the age was *low*, which appears in a new sense soon after 1750, and gives birth to various compounds such as *low-bred* (1757) and *low-lived* (1760). Many persons regarded the growing " delicacy " with some concern. In the Preface to *The Good-Natured Man*, Goldsmith " hopes that too much refinement will not banish humour and character from ours, as it has already done from the French theatre," and Horace Walpole writes sarcastically in 1776, " She lay at home, or, according to the chaste modern phrase, slept there." But the movement continued. *Respectable* assumes its present meaning soon after 1750 ; the modern use of *disreputable* develops during the century, and is established by 1772. Such are a few of the more significant changes in language at a time when manners and class-distinctions were closely scrutinized. A more curious inquiry would reveal matter enough on which to build a whole social chronicle. For example, the appearance of *grand tour*, *watering-place* and *continental* between 1740 and 1760 tell their own story; so does a series belonging to the latter part of the century—*sea-beach*, *sea-view*, *sea-bath* and *sea-scape*. But such developments, however interesting, belong properly to the province of the social historian.

V

To trace the growth of our vocabulary for aesthetic and verbal criticism, we must naturally look to the works of certain eminent writers. As we have seen, many technical terms of literary criticism were introduced by Puttenham and other writers of the late Sixteenth Century. But the critics of that age did not advance far beyond the rudiments of their art. They went to school to the ancients, whose standards they sought to apply, and whose terms they borrowed. Some progress in criticism was made along different lines in the next century, when the merits of Italian art began to be recognized with an enthusiasm more independent than the formal worship of the Classics. Charles I led the taste in painting, and was, to use a new word of the century, a great *virtuoso*. Virtuosity preceded criticism in England. The lovers of contemporary art and music prepared the way for a reasoned attitude in general aesthetics and literary criticism. In virtue of Dryden's *Prefaces*, the Restoration deserves to be called a critical age—at least, in comparison with those which preceded it. But credit is also due to the *virtuosi* of the earlier generation, of whom John Evelyn, the diarist, is the most noteworthy. His lifelong interest in the arts, and his varied accomplishments gave him skill to adopt a number of words without which our language would be much poorer. The following is a roughly chronological list of various words which Evelyn borrowed from French or Italian between 1644 and 1700 : *opera*, " *arcado*," *crayon*, *lampoon*, *pastel*, *contour*, *campanile*, *attitude* (originally a technical term in the arts of design), *vista*. Evelyn was one of the first persons to observe the picturesque effects of mountain-scenery, and he coined the word *alpestral*. Still more interesting is his early use of the word *romantic* in a sense which was later to become common. Writing in 1654 of " the rock of St. Vincent " near Bristol, he remarks : " There is also on the side of this horrid Alp a very romantic seat." Evelyn was a conscious improver of the language and studied its deficiencies. He notes in 1665, " We have hardly any words that do so fully express the French *naivete*, *ennui*, *bizarre*, *concert*."

The vocabulary of aesthetic and intellectual criticism

is not a large one, but its close correspondence with literary history gives it a special interest. Dryden coined *witticism* on the analogy of " criticism," and hazarded the noun *foreground* and the verb *aggroup* in his *Art of Painting*. The French *verve* seems to have been introduced by him. The first record of *action* in the sense " what is done in a poem, drama, etc." occurs in Addison, who appears also to have given *consistency* its current meaning, and to have introduced the words *egotism* and *egotist*, as well as the useful phrase *republic of letters*. Pope, who specially studied the comic effects of bathos, introduced *anticlimax*. Swift's principal addition to the language is a series of proper names borrowed from *Gulliver's Travels*, e.g., *Lilliputian*, *Brobdingnagian*, *Yahoo*, etc., but the first known use of *truism* is also found in his writings, and if he really invented this word, it is a characteristic creation. Another possible creation of Swift's is *party-man*. In the novels of the age may be found various traces of a new vocabulary designed to express both the popular cult of " fine feeling " or " sensibility," and a nice discrimination of character, temperament and behaviour. Richardson's *overanxious* and *aguishly affected* in *Pamela* are examples of this new diction, and his use of *vociferated* in reporting dialogue, as a variant of the monotonous " said " or " cried " with which Defoe was generally content, anticipates a movement which in the modern novel has been carried at least far enough. *Sensibility* has been traced back to an essay of Addison (*Spectator*, No. 231), where Modesty is defined as a " quick and delicate *Feeling* of the soul. It is such an exquisite sensibility, as warns her to shun the first appearance of everything that is hurtful." *Sentimental* in the sense of " exhibiting refined and elevated feeling " occurs as early as 1749 ; but an equal importance may be attached to the first record of the noun *sentiment* in Sterne's *Sentimental Journey* (1768). *Sentimentality* followed two years later, and *sentimentalist* in 1793. The first known use of *lackadaisical* also occurs in Sterne, and he introduced from French the phrase " to temper the wind to the shorn lamb."

The most conscious effort of the century to influence the language was of course that of Dr. Johnson in his *Dictionary* (1755). The fame of the work was great. It was read ; it was quoted ; and its importance in the history of lexicography has been acknowledged by the highest authorities of our own time. Whether Johnson produced the effects he hoped for is, however, more than doubtful. He complains in the Preface that " Our language has been gradually departing from its original *Teutonick* character, and deviating towards a *Gallick* structure and phraseology, from which it ought to be our endeavour to recal it."

This was true, and a reaction ultimately set in. But the task of renewing the older traditions of our language was beyond the strength of a scholar and critic, even of Johnson's calibre. It was left to the poets of the Romantic Revival to restore the prestige of our older vocabulary, and the example of Johnson's style, which had little enough of the " Teutonic character," remained more potent than his excellent precept. Nor was Johnson permanently successful in his attempt to stigmatize recent words of popular origin. " I have studiously endeavoured," he says, " to collect examples and authorities from the writers before the Restoration, whose works I regard as *the wells of English undefiled*, as the pure sources of genuine diction." Various recent words are accordingly marked in the *Dictionary* as " low." *Coax* is " a low word," so are *frisky, simpleton, fuss. Dodge* " in all senses is low and vulgar." *Shabby* is " a word that has crept into conversation and low writing but ought not to be admitted into the language." On the other hand, old words sometimes receive special commendation. *Doff*, we are told, is " scarcely used except by rustics; yet it is a pure and commodious word." Johnson had the prejudices of the etymologist, and disliked words of obscure or unknown origin. Naturally, his censure fell most heavily on words which were still recognized as recent. But the principle of judging a word by its pedigree is inapplicable in the English language. If *fuss* is censurable for its popular origin, so is *sloven*, so are hundreds more. None the less, Johnson's protests were not untimely. They sharpened men's perception of the difference between slang and pure English, and they co-operated with his example to introduce a habit of stricter formality in language, which was not without its benefits. How great was the authority of the *Dictionary* in its own generation, the spelling of several words bears witness to this day. The form *dirk* replaced the earlier *durk* by Johnson's authority. *Despatch*, as an alternative to *dispatch*, is due to a slip on Johnson's part: ordinarily he used the latter form which is correct, and *despatch* perpetuates what is a mere error of the *Dictionary*. The use of *chestnut*, in place of the older *chesnut*, is also due to Johnson.

VI

The words we have hitherto considered belong mostly to the literary vocabulary; they come within the scope of criticism; to accept or reject them is an act of literary taste; they are landmarks in the intellectual life of the nation, and whether good or bad of their kind they belong to that class of words which Coleridge called " the best part of language." To consider with the same fullness those additions

to the vocabulary which by their very nature admit
of no alternatives is unnecessary. When a language
accepts a foreign name for a foreign object, or admits a
technical term for which there is no native equivalent,
literary criticism can say but little. The word obtains
prescriptive rights as the only name for a new idea or
object. This at least was so before the days of scientific
lexicography : in our own time, it is true, organized
effort may succeed in banishing an unlovely word, as
the substitution of the simple *airman* for the pompous
aviator sufficiently proves. But the cult of foreign
terms for their own sake has been a national craze more
than once in our history, and it was a significant thing
for our language that the most notorious of such
crazes, that of Elizabeth's reign, coincided with an age
of colonial enterprise. When, for instance, the potato
was introduced, it was known by its American name
batata, though the French called it " pomme de terre ";
similarly, the *laburnum* kept its Latin name in England,
but received in Germany the figurative title " Gold-
regen " ("golden rain "). No doubt, most European
languages have adopted or naturalized the native
names for many foreign products, but Elizabethan
England definitely preferred the outlandish word for
its own sake. *Tobacco*, for example, which is found
about 1600, is a corruption of the Spanish " tabaco,"
but it is foreign in appearance (more so, certainly, than

the French " tabac ") and was therefore acceptable.
Tomato (*cir.* 1604) is also pseudo-Spanish, being
altered from the Mexican *tomatl*. *Desperado* (1610)
assuredly passed for Spanish, but according to the
best authority it is " perhaps merely a sonorous re-
fashioning after words in -*ado*." The popularity of
" foreign " words at this time is illustrated by the
long list in which the same spurious termination
occurs, *e.g.*, *ambuscado*, *bravado*, *bastinado*, *barricado*,
carbonado, *stoccado*, *strappado*, and the obsolete
armado,* which have (or would have) in Spanish the
ending -*ada*.

In general the European languages have enriched
their neighbours with terms which indicate a special
prestige in certain spheres of activity. From Holland,
over a long period, we borrowed various seafaring
words : the influx begins in the Middle Ages and continues until the end of our great sea-struggle with the
Dutch in the Seventeenth Century. The following is
a select list of words of this class, arranged in roughly
chronological order : *keel* (a flat-bottomed vessel),
skipper, *veer*, *lighter*, *hoy*, *dock*, *yacht*, *laveer*, *bow*, *sloop*,
boom, *smuggle*. Dutch eminence in art was a later
development, and such words as we borrowed, *e.g.*,
landscape, *easel*, *maulstick*, *sketch*, do not appear before
the Seventeenth Century. The word *Hottentot* is a

* All except *bravado*, are used by Shakespeare.

reminder of Dutch enterprise in colonization, and the military terms *leaguer* and *furlough* entered our language during the struggle between the Netherlands and Spain.

To Italian, above all other languages, we are indebted for the technical vocabulary of Music and the Fine Arts. *Adagio, fantasia, finale, piano, sonata,* are a few of the many musical terms borrowed from Italy ; *fresco, mezzotint, replica, studio,* are specimens of the art-vocabulary which we owe to the same source. To these words must be added a considerable miscellaneous list. *Cicerone, dilettante, incognito, influenza, malaria, magnifico, regatta, umbrella,* are no doubt recognized by most persons as Italian, but there are many other words whose origin is less obvious, *e.g.,* *carnival, charlatan, gazette, muslin, pantaloon, pedal.* A number of the Spanish and Portuguese words which have entered English are first found in the various travel-books of the late Sixteenth and early Seventeenth Centuries : examples are *alligator, banana, disembogue, fetish* and *flamingo* ; other Spanish or Portuguese words adopted about the same time are *cocoa, grandee,* and *negro.* The enterprise of seaman and trader is also commemorated in various words of non-European origin. An interesting early example is *canoe,* from a Haytian word found in use by Columbus. From Malay, *amuck, cockatoo, gong, orang-outang* and

M   E.W.

sago, and certain others, entered English during the Sixteenth and Seventeenth Centuries; and of the many far-travelled words which are found in the Voyages and Histories of the same period may be mentioned *assagai* (Berber), *chocolate* (Mexican), *coffee* (Arabic), *firman* (Persian), *lascar* (Urdu), *salaam* (Arabic), *tomahawk* and *wigwam* (North American).

CHAPTER IX

THE HISTORICAL DEVELOPMENT OF THE VOCABULARY SINCE 1800

THE first feelings with which one surveys the changes which have occurred in the vocabulary during the last century and a half are somewhat mixed. Regret at a certain loss struggles with satisfaction for an indubitable gain. Something of the national character of the language certainly disappears with the passing of the Eighteenth Century ; and the Romantic Revival, which restored a taste for our older poets and their speech, synchronized with the French Revolution, which gave birth to democracy and all its incalculable consequences. The principle of democracy leads sooner or later to the principle of national education ; and although this was not accepted in England until 1870, the transformation which it implies had begun long before. To sum up in a sentence the vast changes which have taken place in Standard English since 1800 is quite impossible. But to name what it has lost is perhaps not so difficult : it has lost unity. That one writer should ever again influence the language as profoundly as Dryden influenced it, or

Addison, or Johnson, is quite unthinkable, for pure literature will never again be as important in every sphere of life as it was in the Seventeenth and Eighteenth Centuries. One reason for this is the loss at the Universities of the monopoly enjoyed by Classical Studies. A second—which is another aspect of the same thing—is the vast development in other spheres of knowledge. The Sciences have diminished the influence of the Classics; specialization in a single study has largely taken the place of a liberal education. The result is that the proportion of technical words in our vocabulary is constantly increasing. Many of these, it is true, remain shut up in the laboratory or text-book, but enough find their way into ordinary life to effect a slow but perceptible change in the speech of everyday. Gone, too, are the days when English was the language of a single kingdom. Spoken in every quarter of the globe, the language of a great Republic as well as of a great Empire, its integrity and its purity are threatened by dangers of which Johnson never dreamed. Nor is the influence of the spoken word any longer restricted by locality. Words and phrases from America are familiar in every town of Britain. Were not the study and teaching of English recognized as a primary obligation, we might well look forward to a future of linguistic anarchy.

These changes are too complex to be referred to any

one cause. They reflect the profound developments which have taken place in our national life during the last five generations. But as the England of the Eighteenth Century would in any case have been destroyed by the Reform Act of 1832, we may begin with the movements which brought about that great change. Of these, the chief was the French Revolution.

I

Most historic movements leave behind them a legacy of words, and the French Revolution was no exception. Europe quickly recognized that there was here a change as deep as any which had occurred since the founding of Christianity. It was, indeed, possible to exaggerate the importance even of this movement, and the attempts made in Paris to date history from 1792 overshot their mark. But in the arts of popular agitation and the use of political catch-words the Revolution was truly original. In the skill with which they swayed the masses by words dimly understood and wholly unanalysed, the orators of the Palais Royal pointed the way to generations of journalists and agitators. For instance, to accuse a statesman of the vague crime of " federalism " was for a few months a certain way of procuring his downfall. The potency of words over the minds of men was revealed in a new and portentous manner.

Many words which once wielded the power of the guillotine are now mere phantoms in the pages of history. But others have survived in common use, though shorn of their sting. *Aristocrat* (1789) and *democrat* (1790) are both Revolution words : about them some memories of class-warfare still linger. One peculiarity of the French Revolution was its endeavour to translate abstract theory into political practice. The result is that many of its favourite terms are in the form proper to general ideas, often ending with the Greek termination *-ism*. The value of such words was twofold. They suggested a philosophical origin, and they helped to bury personal distinctions under wide generalities. In other words, they suited an age of violent doctrinaire politics, they were steeped in the power of mass-suggestion. Our political terms, *Liberal* and *Conservative*, though not introduced into England till some years after, both arose in the latter part of the Revolution. The two words suggest a connection with first principles, and are thus more agreeable to the post-Revolutionary world than mere party labels, like *Whig* and *Tory*. Journalists have long since learnt the double-edged effectiveness in party warfare of words ending in *-ism*.

Words of this kind often found their way into our language through the writings of thinkers who used them to add pungency to their eloquence for or against the Revolution. Several were apparently introduced by Burke. Throughout his career that statesman was adding memorable words and phrases to the language. In his works is first recorded the phrase " representation in Parliament " (1769), and he is also the author of " the dissidence of dissent." (1775.) " Men of light and leading " (1790) is Burke's development of a phrase from Milton. The sense of *chivalry* to indicate " the character of the ideal knight " dates from the exclamation in the *Reflections on the Revolution in France,* "the age of chivalry is gone !" (1790.) *Jacobin* makes its first appearance as an English word in the same work. *Federalism* and *moderantism,* the crimes attributed to the Girondins, are first recorded in Burke's writings (1793), and he also gave a temporary fame in England to the *décadi* of the new calendar (1795). Burke's dread of anarchy is commemorated in the sinister *disorganize,* of which the first-known English use occurs in his expression, " Their ever memorable decree of the 15th of December, 1792, for *disorganizing* every country in Europe." (1793.) The current sense of *diplomacy* dates from the same period (1796), and was also of Burke's introduction. Through other writers, *sansculotte, ancient régime, civism,* and other Revolutionary terms became current in England within a year or two of their appearance in France. The sense that the Revolution was something unprecedented in human affairs is well expressed in a passage from Macaulay's " Essay on Barère ": " The antipathy between (Barère) and us is such, that neither for the crimes of his earlier nor for those of his later life does our language, rich as it is, furnish us with adequate names. It is not easy to give a notion of his conduct in the Convention, without using those emphatic terms, *guillotinade*, *noyade*, *fusillade*, *mitraillade*. It is not easy to give a notion of his conduct under the Consulate and the Empire without borrowing such terms as *mouchard* and *mouton*."

The value to popular journalists of words with a learned sound, and in particular of the termination *-ism*, seems to have been discovered during the Revolution. Coleridge and Southey, in their hot-headed days, invented two words of this kind : *pantisocracy* (a community in which all are equal and all rule), and *aspheterism* (the doctrine that there ought to be no private property). *Terrorism* and *moderatism*, two polemical words of the French Revolution, both appeared in England in 1795 ; and the following century produced a host of similar inflammatory terms with which politicians and journalists have plagued mankind. *Nihilism* appeared in 1817, *socialism* in 1839, *communism* in 1843, *nationalism* in 1844, *Caesarism* in 1857, *opportunism* in 1870, *collectivism* in 1880, *pacifism* in 1901, *syndicalism* in 1907, *defeatism* in

1918. Who can set a limit to the power of mass-suggestion in such words? Who can count the fanatics they have produced, or estimate their value to the unscrupulous journalist? Some words of the class, however, have been beneficently used to denounce evil things. Thus *militarism* was on its first appearance (1864) defined by Garibaldi as " that disease of modern times," and blind enthusiasm for national glory was stigmatized as *chauvinism*, after the name of Nicholas Chauvin, a Napoleonic soldier whose excessive patriotism, after exciting the admiration of his comrades, finally provoked the ridicule of later generations.

II

Changes in language obviously have some connection with the history of civilization. The difficulty is to discover what features of a complex civilization bear most directly on the life of words. Among the many new features of Nineteenth Century England, it would seem that the flow of population towards the towns was one of the most far-reaching in its effect on the vocabulary. For many years after the beginning of the Industrial Revolution, the country dialects slept undisturbed; and in various " regional " novels one may read the record of the unchanging country speech which lasted almost till our own time. But the main tide of life was flowing to the industrial towns, where Standard English, more or less pure, began to obscure or obliterate local words and idioms. Many new fashions in our language are due to the growth of the towns, with their brisker life and their demand for popular education. One may picture the language as uprooted from its native soil and exposed to a new air hostile to many of its finer qualities. On the other hand, the elements of a literary education were soon offered to all : training partly compensated for what tradition was losing.

In the larger towns the pace of life runs quickly ; the craving for excitement demands constant satisfaction. As early as 1800, Wordsworth had connected a taste for " frantic novels " with " the congregation of men in cities " ; and since that time a hundred ways have been sought to stimulate and feed the new appetite. A more violent style comes into vogue ; emphasis disguises what is really commonplace. In 1763, Boswell was rebuked by Johnson for his exaggerated expressions,* but Boswell was merely the forerunner of a movement which Johnson was powerless to check. Early in the Nineteenth Century the word *appalling* makes its appearance, and a certain General Thompson remarks in 1836 that " the newspapers

---

* " Don't, Sir, accustom yourself to use big words for little matters." Boswell's *Johnson*, Ætat. 54.

have reported two or three ' appalling accidents ' already." The once tremendous word *awful* began to be used as a mere intensive about 1834, in which year Lamb quotes the colloquial expression " Something awful " ; and many other adjectives, such as *dreadful* and *ghastly*, have been reduced to the same insignificance. *Astoundingly*, which appears in 1826, seems to have been used from the first with much less than its literal force. *Tremendous* is defined by Johnson as " dreadful ; horrible ; astonishingly terrible " ; its use as " a mere intensive " had established itself by about 1850. The desire for violent effects in works of imagination is characterized by various new words which appear in the course of the century. *Melodrama*, which originally meant " a stage-play with songs interspersed," assumed its present sense early in the last century. The new meaning of *sensation* and *sensational* developed in the 'sixties ; the new meaning of *thrill* and *thriller* in the 'eighties. The degradation of language which began a century ago is known to every reader of modern newspapers. The great terms of literature are levelled down to those of recent formation. Nothing is commoner now than an *epic* flight ; an event fully anticipated is nevertheless *dramatic* ; the most sordid of crimes is a *tragedy*. By daily announcing *crises*, the newspapers have gone a long way towards producing them.

III

About 1800 new words were still carefully scrutinized before being allowed admission into what passed for " good English." Hazlitt, who was the reverse of a pedantic writer, printed in italics any words which he felt to be colloquial, and new words were often submitted to examination by the serious reviews. Conservatism in language is often misguided, and no power on earth can prevent the use of a word which is really needed. But to employ new words for no other reason than that they are new, or to use them without being conscious of their newness, is not a practice one would look for in a writer who respects himself or the language. An unthinking and uncritical love of novelty for its own sake, however, certainly operates widely to-day ; well-educated persons are by no means free from it. The tendency appears in the changed attitude towards words of American origin. The term *Americanism* dates from 1794 ; and its use at least implies a discrimination between native and non-native usage. The reluctance to borrow any expression from America was at first unreasoning ; and perhaps some element of the old prejudice survives in the hostility, still occasionally met with, to *reliable*, which, though found in English as early as 1624, has been strongly condemned as an American word. The

objection to *transpire*,* which was misused in America
as a synonym for " occur," was better founded. During the Nineteenth Century, America contributed
various useful words to our language, *e.g.*, *blizzard*
and *stampede*. From the same source came *corner* (a
commercial term), *bogus*, and *rowdy*. By degrees,
Americanisms were adopted less critically, and sometimes, it would appear, for nothing but their modern
flavour. Thus, the older verb *to dewitt* (from the
name of the Dutch statesman, Cornelius de Witt,
murdered by a mob in 1672) has been superseded by
the American verb *to lynch*. *Caucus* was adopted in
England as a term of political abuse in 1878; and,
from its American origin and misunderstood sense,
has become " a term which partizans fling at the
organizations of their opponents, and disclaim for
their own." Within the last half-century Americanisms have come to symbolize smart business methods,
and general modernity; thus the American *store* is
sometimes preferred to the native *shop*. The love of
novelty for its own sake prepared the way for this influx of occidental words. A phrase significant of the
whole movement is *up-to-date*, which assumed its
current meaning about 1889 and instantly became
popular, though it was branded as " vile slang." How

* The proper meaning of *transpire* is " to escape from
secrecy to notice " (Johnson).

many of the newer Americanisms have come to stay no one can tell, but they are finding their way into our dictionaries in increasing numbers. Some well-wishers of the language hope for a judicious blending of what is best in the two main streams of English. Doubtless, both sides of the Atlantic might borrow profitably from the speech of the other ; but if we are to import American words they should surely be of a better quality than such examples as the much-used *turn down*. English possesses words enough for most purposes, and has no need to borrow from American slang.

IV

The cultivation of the most delicate propriety in language was a feature of certain phases of Victorian life ; and various words survive in our language as a memorial of this fashion. A desire to " whitewash " life spread over the country, partly as a reaction against the licence of Regency manners, partly in deference to Queen Victoria's own example. The newly-enriched commercial classes did much to extend the fashion. The term *middle class* is itself a creation of the age and dates from about 1812 ; and it is noteworthy that in the 'nineties it began sometimes to be used with a shade of depreciation. About 1830, the desire to avoid certain expressions as " inelegant " began often to be pushed to absurd lengths. Ridiculous euphemisms came into use for " trousers," which we find variously termed *ineffables*, *inexplicables* and *unmentionables*. " Leg " was regarded as vulgar, and was often replaced by *limb*. A " naked " figure was more elegantly styled *nude* or *undraped*. French expressions were sometimes introduced to avoid the plain-speaking of native words. Thus *retroussé* (1837) sounds more considerate than " snub " ; *décolleté* (1831) is more refined than " low-necked." As the code of manners became more rigid, and the middle class rose in social consequence, the word *lady* underwent some change in meaning ; previously used of status, it began about 1860 to imply the possession of certain manners, habits and sentiments. In the new refinement of domestic life the small virtues and vexations of the home needed appropriate names, not too emphatic. Thus, *tidy*, though an older word in some senses, came to be the familiar epithet of an orderly house or room in the first half of the century. *Mess*, in the sense of " confusion " or " muddle," is first found about the same time, and another contemporary is *fad* ;* so also is *nuisance*, originally a much stronger word, and now weakened into expressing a mild sense of annoyance. The manners of men were also distinguished by a new set of words. *Cad* was borrowed from University slang about 1840 ;

* Adopted from dialects into general use, about this time.

loud in the sense of "flashy" appears in *Pendennis* (1849), and the whole duty of social man is summed up in the phrase *good form* (1868). To denominate those who indulged in the prevalent vice of toadying to rank and station, Thackeray bestowed a new and useful sense on the word *snob* (1848).

V

The majority of words added to the Dictionary during the Nineteenth Century were words of Classical, and especially of Greek, origin. This is due to the vast development of the physical sciences which, as in the days of Bacon, Boyle and Newton, founded their terminology on Greek and Latin words. Often a whole group of terms is based on a single word, for in every branch of knowledge investigation was carried on by the *specialist* (a word which first appears in the 'sixties). Thus from the single word *seismos* (an earthquake), over twenty derivatives have been formed since 1840. Bishop Blougram in Browning's poem remarks how the increase of Greek terminations signifies the victory over some old "faith" or superstition :

> Greek endings with the little passing-bell
> That signifies some faith's about to die.

It is well for the language that the new technical terms were mostly formed with some regard for scholarship, analogy, and euphony. This is partly due to the broad-mindedness of many of the greatest scientists, *e.g.*, Humphry Davy, Faraday, and Huxley, all of whom deeply respected the "humanities." For instance, the word *aluminium* (1812) assumed its present form after three attempts : Davy tried *alumium*, then *aluminum* ; finally *aluminium* was accepted on a suggestion from the *Quarterly Review*. Similarly, the hybrid *weather-ology* has been superseded by the more correct *meteorology*. The number of scientific words of Greek origin which have entered the language since about 1850 passes computation, but a glance at the *Oxford Dictionary* under any such prefix as *hydro-*, *mega-*, *meso-*, *ortho-*, *palaeo-*, gives some idea of the enormous addition to the technical side of our language.

Many technical words belong to the English Dictionary rather than to the English Language : even the best educated man will never meet more than a fraction of them. But many of the creations of applied science enter into our daily life and thought, and their names become "household words." Some such objects and inventions have assumed names based on the classical languages, *e.g.*, *telegraph*, *sanitation*, but the unlimited multiplication of such words would not

N   E.W.

be desirable, and it seems that a name like the German " Fernsprecher " (literally " distance-speaker ") is in one way preferable to our *telephone*. A popular nickname or label like *steamer* is often the best possible word for its purpose. The development of our railway-vocabulary was particularly fortunate : a number of new objects, which had to be frequently named by a large part of the population, were christened by words which had all the appearance of being native or popular. *Train* is part of the phrase " train of waggons "; *shunt* and *trolley* are borrowed from dialects ; *truck* and *rail* are old-established words with new applications. But to go to the opposite extreme and substitute words of native origin for well-established technical names would be foolish ; though, of course, it is not easy to fix the boundaries between the general and the technical. Suggestions for extending words of Anglo-Saxon origin into the realm of the sciences have, however, been made ; but the advantage of the " learned " element in our language is here revealed with peculiar force. Science is international, and a word like *oxygen* is immediately intelligible in many countries besides England, whereas its German equivalent *Sauerstoff* (" sour-stuff ") seems designed only for national use. To adopt the suggestion which was once made of substituting the " Anglo-Saxon " *birdlore* and *earthlore* for " ornithology " and " ge-

ology," would be to run counter to a principle
established in our language for more than six
centuries.

VI

Technical words, however, are not the best or most
important part of our verbal heritage. The Nineteenth Century, while witnessing an immense growth
of specialized knowledge, gave us also a number of
words which are now indispensable to educated
thought and writing. Many such words derive a
special interest from the thinkers with whom they are
associated, and some even bring before us the outline
of an intellectual portrait. For example, *publicist* is not
found in English until it appears in a writing of Burke
(1792), who is himself the prince of publicists. To
Jeremy Bentham we owe *international, self-regarding,
minimize*, and perhaps *unilateral, confederative, detach-
able, exhaustive*, and various others. Coleridge, in
his prose-writings, was a great coiner of words. Some
are formed rather recklessly, others are useful additions
to the language. Historically seen, his vocabulary
mirrors a ceaseless exploration among the " countries of the mind." Many of his formations though
only derivatives from existing words are suggestive
and useful, *e.g., actualize, associative, catholicity, contextual, intensify, relativity, transitional*. He is also

credited with *other-worldliness*, *realism* and (in an obsolete sense) *pessimism*. Though some of these words may possibly be traced back to an earlier date, Coleridge certainly did much to give them currency, and as a group they reveal his effort to enrich our philosophical vocabulary. *Elizabethan*, of which the first example in the *Oxford Dictionary* is a quotation from Coleridge (1817), has since been traced back to a somewhat earlier writer ; but it is in any case a landmark in the growth of that historical sense which is a feature of the Nineteenth Century. The phrase *spirit of the age* which has a similar significance is first recorded in Shelley (1820). *Renaissance*, adopted about 1840, shows that the need was felt of adopting a wider and also handier expression than the cumbrous " revival of learning." So, too, *mediaeval* (1827) supplies the want of an adjective corresponding to " Middle Ages." These are but a few examples indicating the spread of a historical outlook. The same tendency is shown in the adoption of more accurate spellings : thus *Tsar* replaces the older *Czar*, *Serbian* replaces *Servian* ; native racial terms such as *Czech* (1841) and *Vlach* (1841) come into use beside the older " Bohemian " and " Walachian " ; and as a result of this process, spellings like Macaulay's *Lewis* for the French *Louis* now strike the reader as curious. Another feature of the Nineteenth Century was the growth of Science and the increasing number of persons who devoted themselves to scientific pursuits. A notable gap in the vocabulary was filled when the word *scientist* was deliberately coined by William Whewell (1840). Various philosophies and theories, too, were named by their founders; and possibly some such words will outlive the memory of their creators. *Agnostic* was suggested by T. H. Huxley in 1869; *altruism* was formed by the French philosopher, Comte, and introduced into English by G. H. Lewes (1853); *determinism* seems to be the creation of Sir William Hamilton (1846). In their purely linguistic aspect some recent words illustrate the common habit of the age to form new abstract or general terms with Greek and Latin terminations. There is, for instance, a large group of such words beginning with *de-* and ending with *-ize*: *e.g.*, *denationalize* (1807), *denaturalize* (1812), *demonetize* (1852), *depauperize* (1863), *demobilize* (1882), *dematerialize* (1884). The introduction of such words in large numbers is a source of danger to the purity of the language, and they are often used to give an official or pseudo-scientific air to a plain matter which might be described simply. For instance, *demobilize* has, in recent years, almost entirely replaced the older *disband*. The tendency seems to illustrate the instinct of officialdom to force itself on the passive mind of the

masses, and to involve the processes of government
in mystery.

VII

The docile acceptance during the last fifty years or
so of technical and " official " words is partly a reaction from the ways of the earlier generation. A
language of great poetic wealth, developed by the
inventiveness of the past, needs a strong tradition of
criticism and scholarship to control it. In the first
half of the Nineteenth Century, the right of poetry
to free expression was reasserted with great force;
but the corresponding need for continuity with the
best usage of the past was a matter which excited
much less interest. As a result, various writers of
great power indulged in all sorts of caprice : there
was no Academy, no organized authority, no adequate dictionary to check them. The supreme example of this combination of genius with licence
was Carlyle, who corrupted the language which he
also enriched. Carlyle's prose abounds in verbal
novelties : how many of them can be called new
" words," how many are mere freaks of style is still
debatable. Certain verbs formed by the simple addition of a prefix and designed to add a touch of humour
to some description, *e.g.*, *dishero*, recall the licence of
the Jacobean drama, but lack the same excuse of an

accepted tradition. Some of his adjectives are on the borderline, or have even taken the status of " words " : examples are *affordable, adoptable, dislikable, forgettable*; but *redtapist* is a pure freak. Of his numerous formations from Latin, some have the appearance of "noncewords," *e.g., fremescent, languescent,* and *palpitant,* but *decadent* has been adopted, though its meaning has somewhat changed. The Greek *eleutheromania* is a typical formation, and it is not without excuse in a historian of the French Revolution. From the Scottish element in Carlyle's prose, *outcome* has entered the general vocabulary. His figurative use of *wind-bag* as " a senseless talker " has also been adopted. So has *formulism,* which expresses his hatred of " shams," and he has given a new meaning to *formula,* which is illustrated in the sentence : " Man lives not except with formulas ; with customs, ways of doing and living." These examples are enough to show the nature of Carlyle's influence on the language, which was due as much to his forcible individuality as to his verbal skill. His example was sometimes followed by other writers, and Ruskin's *illth* (1860), the reverse of " wealth," recalls Carlyle's manner. The half-humorous recklessness of Carlyle was also anticipated by some slightly earlier writers, and Sydney Smith's *noodledom,* which was adopted by Browning, calls to mind Carlyle's fondness for old English affixes.

" Lewis Carroll " is another inventor of freak-words, but a few, *e.g.*, *chortle*, are really useful formations.

The occasional recklessness to which certain Victorians must plead guilty was characteristic of the times, but it was scrupulously avoided by some of their contemporaries. Tennyson was free from it ; Arnold denounced it. Moreover, in the long run, it is the abuser of the language, not the language itself, that suffers.

VIII

We have considered some of the defects of Nineteenth Century English, and have yet to deal with the forces which renewed the finer spirit of the language and have preserved many of its best qualities to the present day. To the Romantic Revival and its consequences English owes an incalculable debt ; and among the writers of that movement it is particularly indebted to Scott, Wordsworth and Coleridge. These men could never have done their work without a conception of language far broader than that which they inherited from the previous age. Wordsworth's passion for truth and simplicity, Scott's vision of the past, Coleridge's imaginative daring, demanded, each for its own purposes, the unused resources of our vocabulary. In old books, or in " the real language of men," these writers discovered a wealth of beauty unknown to the pages of Johnson's *Dictionary*. Of the Romantic writers, Scott brought the greatest number of new words—or rather, of old words stranded in dialects or hidden in books—into the living language, but the poetic example of Wordsworth and the philosophic criticism of Coleridge were not less potent. Coleridge helped to destroy the view promoted by Johnson that pre-Restoration English was " a language of brick," converted by Dryden into "a language of marble," and one of his main achievements as a critic was to show that many poets of the early Seventeenth Century were, with all their faults, true artists in expression. In Lamb's work, too, the beauty of Elizabethan English lives again ; the language of the old drama is woven into the texture of his style. Hazlitt uses a vocabulary at once newer and older than Dr. Johnson's, and De Quincey reveals in some skilful criticism the felicity of Shakespeare's boldest language. At the same time, the foundations of a historical study of English were being laid by writers imbued with the same love of the past. A scholar here and an antiquary there were beginning to show that the native elements of the language were worthy of systematic study, that Anglo-Saxon has a history no less than Greek and Latin. The great attention which has since been paid to the Teutonic elements of English is partly an outcome of the Romantic Movement.

Scott's art both as poet and novelist lay partly in his use of a vocabulary which recalled the picturesque past and preserved the memories of feudal Scotland. He was deeply read in the old drama and ballads, and familiar with the Border dialect. Words and phrases collected from a vast miscellaneous reading are scattered over his pages in careless profusion. For minute accuracy he cares little, and yet, in essentials, he has the spirit of a great historian. To represent the full extent to which English is indebted to his influence is impossible, for such things cannot be nicely calculated. But a few instances of the revived words which are first recorded in his works will suggest both the nature of his studies and the spell he exercised on the minds of his readers. No word to which Scott has given general currency is more typical than *glamour*. Originally a northern corruption of " grammar," its sense was transformed by the superstition of an age which confused learning with magic, and it came to mean " a spell." It is so used by Scott; but passing through the alchemy of romance which he himself did much to create, it finally assumed the meaning of " alluring charm." It was the " glamour " of Scott's revivals that made them so acceptable. *Damozel*, *glaive* (a sword), *orgillous* (proud), *outrecuidance* (arrogance)—such are the archaisms which give the style of Scott and of his followers its romantic flavour.

These words were current in earlier English. Another group consists of words drawn from the Scottish Lowlands. Most of these have remained dialectal; but a few have been adopted from Scott into literary English: such are *gruesome*, *raid*, and (perhaps) the disparaging sense in which *canny* is applied to the proverbial caution of the North. *Free lance*, a title for the military adventurer who sold his services, is first recorded in *Ivanhoe* (1820); *fabliau*, introduced by Scott in 1804, commemorates his reading in Old French. Shakespearian phrases abound in the *Waverley Novels*, and it is apparently by this route that some of them have entered ordinary English. Two examples are *coign of vantage* (*Macbeth*, 1, vi, 7), and *towering passion* (*Hamlet*, v, ii, 80). The useful verb *smoulder*, which was current in the Sixteenth Century, fell out of use between 1600 and 1800; but it is revived in *The Lady of the Lake* (" Still ... smoulders in Roderick's breast the feud "), and thereafter again becomes common. *Stalwart*, a Sixteenth Century Scottish form of " stalworth," entered English from the same poem (" Whose stalwart arm might brook to wield A blade like this in battle-field "). Another old word which Scott familiarized is *foray*, and he renewed the life of the obsolescent *onslaught*. Scott did not create the appetite for romance, but he eclipsed all rivals in his own field. In the romance of the Near East, Byron was no less supreme, but the Oriental terms which he introduced to add colour to his poems * did not, like many of Scott's words, find their way into the ordinary vocabulary. Byron had none of Scott's power of anticipating the needs of future historians and writers of romantic fiction.

IX

In his definition of poetry as " the best words in the best order," Coleridge suggests one of the chief functions which poets have to fulfil. Loyalty to the highest demands of their art is a service not only to themselves but to the language which they use. English owes a great debt to many poets of the Nineteenth Century, who by seeking to use permanent expressions did much to preserve the language at a time when it was liable to rapid change. The power of poetry whether for good or ill had, however, much contracted since the Seventeenth Century. As learning and science had advanced, the scope of the poet had decreased. Though much was written about the function of the poet as *vates* or hero, it was the tendency of the age to make poetry a fine art rather than a creative art, and it is for this reason that Tennyson is the most representative poet of the time. Poetry still had its own

* See p. 107.

idiom and vocabulary, more consciously indeed than ever before, but the words of poetry were often distinguished by shades of usage too subtle for the dictionary to register. The new poetic coinages of the age were for the most part descriptive and fanciful—at the best suggestions for other poets, and seldom contributions to the general vocabulary. Few poets of the age ever approached, as Browning often does, the idiom of ordinary life. On the contrary, many persons read poetry principally from a desire to escape from the prose of the " modern " world. The past, especially the mediaeval past, was found to be more " poetic " than the Nineteenth Century. This discovery had a natural influence upon language. There was a cult of Anglo-Saxon diction which affected the style of various " romantic " writers. Thus *leechcraft*, the old word for the art of healing, was revived by Scott and repeated by Lytton and Morris. A few words still linger in the language as a memorial of the times when " our homely Saxon " was praised for its directness and virility, and critics of style deplored the intrusion of sophisticated alien words. A certain vogue has been, and still is, enjoyed by *foreword*, an " English " equivalent of the German *Vorwort*, intended to supersede the 500-years-old " preface." The first example of *foreword* is dated 1842. Four years later we find *folk-lore* recommended as " a good Saxon compound." This movement was in part poetical: even so great a master of language as Tennyson occasionally impoverishes his style by excluding non-native words. William Morris, whose poetic gifts did not always protect him from harmful theories, goes to greater lengths, and revives words of Anglo-Saxon and Norse origin with an effect which is sometimes grotesque. Such is the result of his rendering νεφεληγερέτα Ζεύς (cloud-compelling Jupiter) as "the god that driveth the lift." None the less, the union of poetic talent with philological knowledge in Morris produced notable results, and his love of Old Norse and Anglo-Saxon helped to give a literary interest to studies which might have remained simply antiquarian.

Victorian poetry performed a great service to the language by its alliance with scholarship and education. Tennyson, in particular, possessed not only the poet's love of beauty, but the scholar's care for accurate usage. Often experimental, he showed a wonderful sense for the varied origins of the language, and could draw on all its resources with a knowledge which was equal to his artistic instinct. When the weakening of tradition in an era of change was threatened by ignorance, pedantry and wild individualism, Tennyson's diction remained aloof and electic, and his example remained effective for half a century. Pursuing his own path, Matthew Arnold performed a similar service to the language, and it is perhaps in our generation rather than in his own that his work has borne fruit. His high conception of criticism: "a disinterested endeavour to learn and propagate the best that is known and thought in the world," his severity towards "provinciality" of manner and matter, his keen analysis of the verbal defects in various translations of Homer, were all part of a lifelong effort to raise the use of English to a higher level, and to make the reading public conscious of the qualities required in a "classical" style. Another artist in both prose and verse, whose readers can scarcely fail to gain a quickened sense of the power of language when handled by skill and learning, is Stevenson. For words with a history he had the passion of a collector, and he used them with something of the delicate care which marks the art of his contemporary, Pater. Nor is Stevenson timidly conservative: he affects new or rare derivatives from Latin, such as *desipient*, *desistance*, and he is perhaps the creator of that useful adjective *amoral*. Of all the scholar-poets, the most conscious of his duty towards the language was the late Laureate, Robert Bridges. A master of accomplished verse, he was also a fine critic of contemporary usage, and his concern for the future of the language prompted him to take a leading part in the formation of the Society for Pure English. He endeavours, in certain parts of his latest poem, *The Testament of Beauty*, to reconcile poetry with the technical language of science. The attempt is not wholly successful : but it is a matter of great significance that a poet should seek to weave into one harmony words of beauty with words of use. The more completely life and poetry interpenetrate each other, the better it will be for the whole of our culture.

X

Poets can do much to renew and invigorate the life of language. But something more is required than the incalculable forces of genius : language needs the care of co-operating intelligence. The most important problem for the vocabulary is the best method of creating, adopting and assimilating new words. Over a century ago Jeremy Bentham made a plea for deliberate word-creation. " For characterising an object which not only is new, but is designed to be presented as such, a word as plainly new is much more convenient than any old word taken from the old-established stock of words belonging to the language." In some departments of life this recommendation is superfluous; and, as we have already seen, " trade-names " are introduced into the language with the utmost freedom, to live or die as the state of the market decrees. Nor have the sciences been backward in increasing their special terminology. The chief problem seems to arise over the manner of increasing the intellectual words belonging to the common stock. Examples have already been quoted of words deliberately coined by Huxley and others ; but in a world where new ideas pass rapidly over the frontiers between nation and nation, it is often more natural to adopt some foreign word already in use. Thus the Russian word *intelligentsia* began to be used in England about 1914, and the existence of a term to denote " the class consisting of the educated portion of the population " has proved highly convenient, though its want was apparently not intolerable before. French, as being the foreign language best known in England, has been our chief creditor, and as its genius is essentially different from that of English, it has been able to contribute an immense number of useful words. In certain departments of life the terms of French origin are quite indispensable : how, for instance, could the theatre do without *matinée*, *début*, *rôle*, *dénouement* ? So, too, the language of intellectual discussion would be poorer without such terms as *milieu*, *aperçu* and *nuance* ; occasionally the English writer thinks with envy of certain French words, *e.g.*, the verb *préciser*, which would neatly express his meaning if only he could use them. No stylist, however, feels quite at ease in using many words

O

which are self-declared as foreign, both by their pronunciation and their italics. Occasionally the remedy
is simple. The writer, for instance, who objects to
repertoire has merely to use *repertory*, which is in fact
the older word of the two. Had *Renascence* been proposed in 1840 instead of 1869, it might have preserved
the language from the foreign and unnatural *Renaissance*; but twenty-nine years of life had established
the latter form too firmly. Complete naturalization
may at times take place if an English pronunciation is
adopted. Thus, the sounding of the final -*t* in *trait*
may be American, but it is also in consonance with
older English practice. Sometimes, however, the
vowel-sounds present an insuperable difficulty. The
bold suggestion of Robert Bridges that *timbre* should
be converted into " tamber " seems to have provoked
much resentment when it was once tentatively used,
and similar changes would certainly outrage educated
opinion. Naturalization in some form, however, is
desirable ; and the Society for Pure English is right
to protest against " the false ideal of correctness,
which regards the foreign forms of borrowed words
as the right forms, and which impedes their assimi-
lation." There is much to be said for the use of
certain spellings, still comparatively rare, *e.g.*, *naïvety*
and *revery* for *naïveté* and *reverie*. The purist is sometimes tempted to congratulate himself on the compara-

tive ignorance of most foreign languages in England. Thus Carlyle was forced, in 1831, to introduce the German " Zeitgeist " in the form of *time-spirit*, and in 1903, Mr. G. B. Shaw gave us *superman* for " Übermensch." Both of these are adequate and convenient words. Knowledge of German, however, has grown since Carlyle's time, and " Zeitgeist " is now, not infrequently, used as an " English " word.

That a language should borrow foreign ideas when they are needed is of course desirable ; but that it should be unable to naturalize the words it borrows is disquieting. The days are gone when English would quickly transform any foreign word it needed into an easy and convenient shape, *e.g.*, the German " Lärche " into *larch*, or " Flügelmann " into *fugleman*. Something of this power revived for a short time during the Great War ; but the forces of " education " are too strong for such a thing to last. The belief is not yet dead that foreign languages have their own laws and historic character, but that English is too generous to assert its own nature, or has no definite nature to assert.

The traditional life of the language has been weakening for more than a century, and education has scarcely awakened to its responsibilities. This is the more deplorable seeing how well scholarship has prepared the way for the teacher. Thanks to the labours of James

Murray, Henry Bradley, and the many scholars who both preceded and followed them, English has now the greatest dictionary that any language has ever possessed. This dictionary can and should become a great instrument in higher education. The history and usage of every word known since the beginning of Middle English down to the present time are recorded with an accuracy and fullness which make our language one of the best-mapped provinces of all knowledge. Yet the authority of the dictionary is unrecognized even by thousands of persons who in some sense or other are linguists. Its value as a companion to our literature, and as a guide to certain branches of our history—especially the history of ideas—has yet to be fully exhibited. Above all, the dictionary has a signal part to play in preserving the continuity of the language, and so ensuring that change may take place without debasement. In the intellectual life of a nation, the condition of its language is not the least important matter. The past of English has not been inglorious; its future rests largely in the hands of the teacher.

XI

Since the publication of the *Oxford English Dictionary* began in 1883, much new matter has accumulated for record. Fuller knowledge of the earlier periods of the language, and the natural growth of the vocabulary provided material enough for a large *Supplement.* This was published in 1933, and it is a striking illustration both of the high level of lexicography in England and of the most recent developments of the language. Unfortunately, there is more ground for satisfaction on the first head than on the second. The quality of the latest contributions to the vocabulary has been adversely criticized, and not without reason. Lovers of the language, however, are entitled to remember that half a century is relatively a small period in the life of English, which has a tradition of culture dating from the time of King Alfred. None the less, the past entails a responsibility on the present. If it is the genius of English to be " free " rather than " strict," its character and usage should be all the more scrupulously respected. If its readiness to borrow has given it great variety and wealth, unnecessary additions should not be allowed to drive well-established words out of use. The diffusion of the language over so large a part of the earth may well threaten its finer qualities. Admitting so much, it is perhaps allowable to feel at times something of the hope and enthusiasm with which the Elizabethan poet, Daniel, made his remarkable prophecy :

> And who in time knowes whither we may vent
>   The treasure of our tongue, to what strange shores
>   This gain of our best glorie shall be sent,
> T' inrich unknoweing Nations with our stores ?
> What worlds in th' yet unformed Occident
> May come refin'd with th' accents that are ours ?

INDEX

PRINTED IN GREAT BRITAIN
BY ROBERT MACLEHOSE AND CO. LTD.
THE UNIVERSITY PRESS, GLASGOW